BABIES
& OTHER HAZARDS OF SEX

BABIES

& OTHER HAZARDS OF SEX

How to make a tiny person in only 9 months, with tools you probably have around the home

DAVE BARRY

Illustrated by Jerry O'Brien

Rodale Press, Emmaus, Pennsylvania

Printed in the United States of America on recy-cled paper containing a high percentage of de-inked fiber.

Book design by Anita Groller

Library of Congress Cataloging in Publication Data
Barry, Dave.
    Babies and other hazards of sex.

    Includes index.
    1. Parenting—Anecdotes, facetiae, satire, etc. 2. Childbirth—Anecdotes, facetiae, satire, etc. 3. Infants—Anecdotes, facetiae, satire, etc. 4. Child development—Anecdotes, facetiae, satire, etc. I. Title.
HQ755.8.B38   1984   649′.1   84-11526
ISBN 0-87857-510-3   paperback

    15 17 19 20 18 16 14   paperback

Contents

Author's Qualifications to Write a Book about Babies

Dave Barry, 36, has a son, Robert, who began as a baby and successfully reached the age of 3 without becoming an ax murderer or anything, as far as anybody knows.

In addition, Mr. Barry has spent a number of hours thinking about babies, and has observed them in other people's cars at traffic lights. He also owns a dog, and at the age of 15 completed much of the course required to obtain a Red Cross Senior Lifesaving Badge.

Chapter 1

Should You Have a Baby? Should Anybody?

UNPREGNANT WOMAN
(PROBABLY WILL REMAIN
UNPREGNANT, TOO)

PREGNANT WOMAN

Some Important Pompous Advice to Couples about to Get Pregnant

Getting pregnant is an extremely major thing to do, especially for the woman, because she has to become huge and bloated and wear garments the size of café awnings. This is the woman's job, and it is a tradition dating back thousands of years to a time when men were not available for having babies because they had to stand outside the cave night and day to fend off mastodons.

Of course, there is very little mastodon-fending to be done these days, but men still manage to keep themselves busy, what with buying tires and all. So it is still pretty much the traditional role of the woman to get pregnant and go through labor and have the baby and feed it and nurture it up until it is

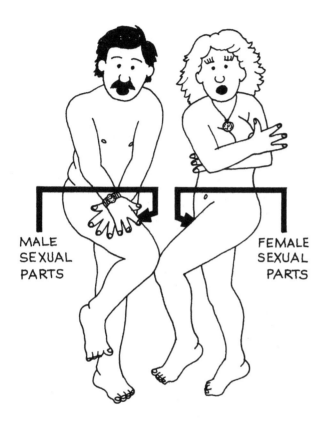

MALE
SEXUAL
PARTS

FEMALE
SEXUAL
PARTS

old enough to throw a football with reasonable accuracy.

In recent years, however, men have become more involved in childbirth and childrearing as part of a federally mandated national trend. Under the terms of this trend, men are beginning to see that they can free themselves from the restrictions of their self-made macho prisons and allow themselves to show their emotions openly—to laugh, to cry, to love, to just generally behave like certified wimps. What this means to you males is that if you get a female pregnant, you are now expected to behave in an extremely sensitive manner and watch the baby come out. I will explain how to do this later.

My point here, young couples, is that baby-having is extremely serious business, and you probably don't have the vaguest idea what you're doing, as is evidenced by the fact that you're reading a very sloppy and poorly researched book. So I think you should start off with the quiz on the opposite page to test your knowledge of important baby facts.

Male Birth Control

To understand the problems involved in birth control, let's look at this quotation from the excellent 1962 medical reference work *Where Do Babies Come From?*, which I purchased from a nurse at a yard sale:

"The way the rooster gets his sperm inside the hen, to fertilize her egg, is very strange to us."

The problem with this quotation, of course, is that it suggests we have given a great deal of thought to the question of how to get sperm inside a chicken. But it does

Quiz for Young Couples Who Want to Have a Baby and Who Clearly Have No Idea What They're Getting Into

1. HOW MANY TIMES DO YOU ESTIMATE THAT A BABY'S DIAPER MUST BE CHANGED BEFORE THE BABY BECOMES TOILET TRAINED?

a. One million billion jillion.

b. One skillion hillion drillion gazillion.

c. Many babies never become toilet trained.

2. WHAT IS THE MOST DISGUSTING THING YOU CAN IMAGINE THAT A BABY MIGHT DELIBERATELY PUT INTO ITS MOUTH?

a. A slime-covered slug.

b. A slime-covered slug that has just thrown up all over itself.

c. A slime-covered slug that has just thrown up all over itself because it has fallen into a vat of toxic sewage.

3. WHEN IS THE BEST TIME TO TAKE A BABY TO A NICE RESTAURANT?

a. During a fire.

b. On Easygoing Deaf People's Night.

c. After the baby has graduated from medical school.

4. WHAT DO YOU DO IF YOUR TWO-MONTH-OLD BABY IS SCREAMING IN AN AIRPLANE AND REFUSES TO SHUT UP AND IS CLEARLY DISTURBING THE OTHER PASSENGERS?

a. Summon the stewardess and say: "Stewardess, whose baby is this?"

b. Summon the stewardess and say: "Stewardess, this baby is very interested in aviation. Please take it up and show it around the cockpit for the duration of the flight."

c. Summon the stewardess and say: "Stewardess, please inform the captain that this infant has just handed me a note in which it threatens to continue crying unless it is taken to Havana immediately."

HOW TO SCORE   Give yourself one point for each question you answered. If you scored three or higher, you are very serious about this, and you might as well go ahead and have a baby. If you scored two or lower, you either aren't really interested in having a baby, or you have the I.Q. of a tree stump. In either case, you should read the section on birth control.

Those of you who are going to have babies should skip the sections on birth control, because they contain many sexually explicit terms, such as "rooster." You can go directly to the section, "How Much Does It Cost to Have a Baby?"

bring up the basic issue in birth control, which is to avoid fertilization you somehow have to keep the male sperm away from the female egg. This is not easy, because men contain absurd quantities of sperm, produced by the same hormone that causes them to take league softball seriously.

The most effective method of birth control for males is the one where, just when the male and the female are about to engage in sex, the friends of the male burst out of the bushes and yell and jump up and down on the bumper and spray shaving cream all over the car. The problem is that this

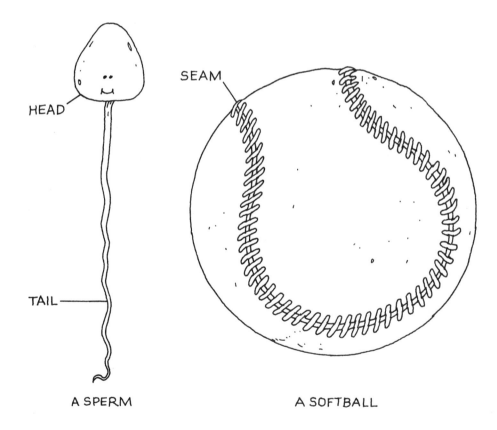

A SPERM   A SOFTBALL

method is pretty much limited to teenage males. Another popular form of teenage birth control is the condom, which the male uses by placing it in his wallet and carrying it around for four years and pulling it out to show his friends in the Dairy Queen parking lot.

I'LL NEED AT LEAST 3 PIECES OF IDENTIFICATION!

THE CONDOM LADY

STANDARD CONDOM

MEXICAN CONDOM

When I was a teenage male, it was very difficult to obtain condoms, because you had to buy them at the drugstore from the Condom Lady, who was about 65 and looked like your grandmother only more moral. She had a photographic memory so she knew exactly who you were, and as soon as you left the store, she would dial a special number that would connect her with a gigantic loud-

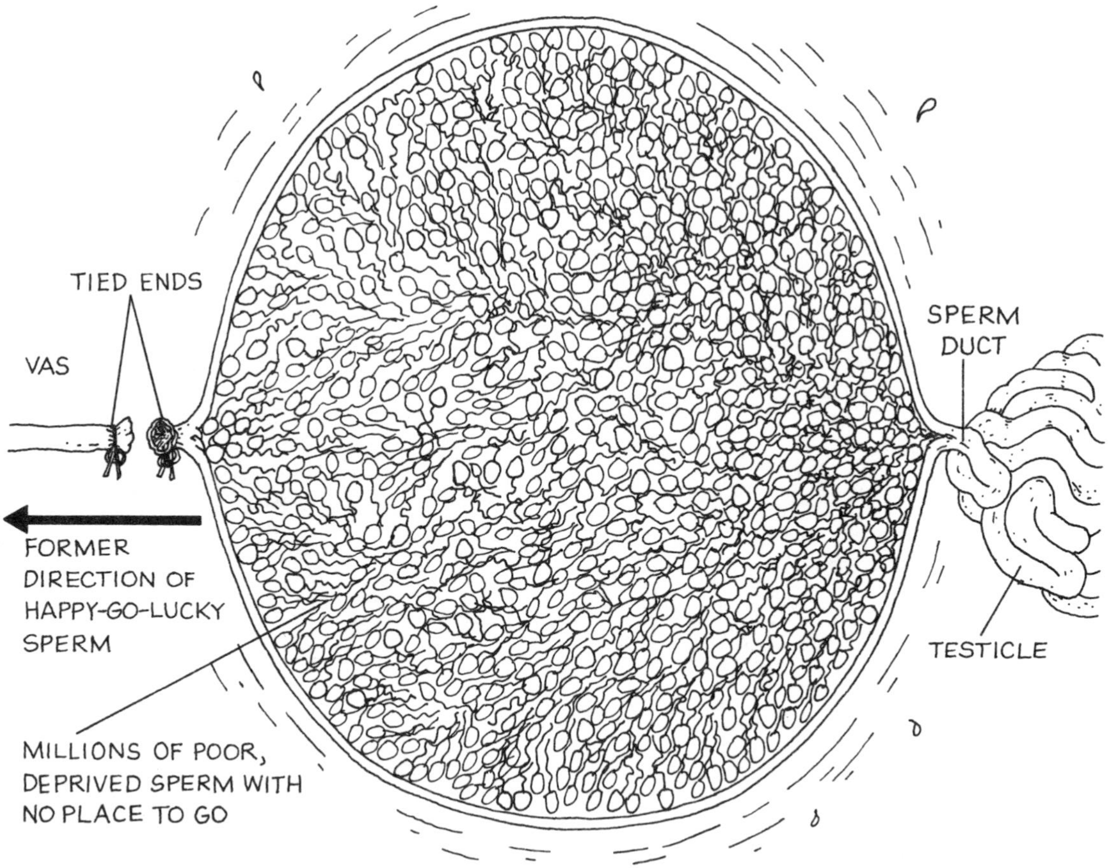

THE AFTERMATH OF A TYPICAL VASECTOMY

TIED ENDS

VAS

SPERM DUCT

FORMER DIRECTION OF HAPPY-GO-LUCKY SPERM

TESTICLE

MILLIONS OF POOR, DEPRIVED SPERM WITH NO PLACE TO GO

speaker system so she could announce to your parents and your teachers and everybody in your church or synagogue and people on the street that you had just bought condoms. Now they sell condoms right out in the open on display racks, just like breath mints or something, and the Condom Lady has switched over to selling *Penthouse* magazine to middle-aged businessmen at the airport.

For older males, the most effective form of birth control is the vasectomy, which is a simple surgical procedure that can be done right in your doctor's office. Notice I say *your* doctor's office. I myself would insist on having it done at the Mayo Clinic surrounded by a team of several dozen cracker-jack surgeons and leaders of all the world's major religious groups. I don't take any chances with so-called minor surgical procedures, because the last one I had was when the dentist took my wisdom teeth out, and subsequently I almost bled to death in the carpet department at Sears.

The way I understand it, what happens in a vasectomy is they tie some kind of medical knot in the male conduit so the sperm can't get through. Of course, this leads to the obvious question, which is: Won't the sperm back up? Will these poor pathetic males someday explode like water balloons, spewing sperm all over and possibly ruining an important sales presentation? I say the American Medical Association ought to get the hell off the golf course and answer this question before the public becomes needlessly alarmed.

Female Birth Control

Female birth control is much more complicated, because once sperm are safely inside a female, they become very aggressive. They barge up and down the various feminine tubes and canals, hooting and whistling, until they locate the egg. Then they strike up a conversation, feigning great interest in the egg's personality, but actually looking for the first opportunity to penetrate.

There is no absolutely foolproof way to stop this fertilization process. The old wives'

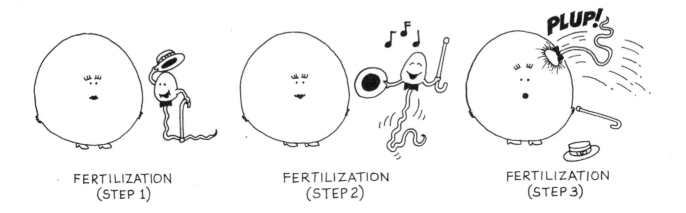

FERTILIZATION
(STEP 1)

FERTILIZATION
(STEP 2)

FERTILIZATION
(STEP 3)

tale, of course, is that a female could avoid getting pregnant by not having sex, but this was disproved by a recent experiment in which Harvard University biologists placed 50 old wives in a locked condominium for two years, and 35 percent of them got pregnant anyway merely by looking at pictures of Raymond Burr.

But there are things that a woman can do. She can insert one of the many feminine insertion devices shaped like alien space vehicles, which are designed to scare the sperm into stampeding right back out the

vestibule. Or she can take the pill, which messes with her hormones in such a way that her body gets fooled into thinking it is already pregnant. The egg gets all bloated and starts to feel weepy and nauseous in the morning, and when it comes clomping down the fallopian tubes, the sperm all go stampeding right back out the vestibule.

What the public is eagerly awaiting, of course, is a birth-control pill for males. If you ever see members of the public gathering in eager little knots, that's what they're waiting for. The male medical establishment has been assuring us for years that such a pill is right around the corner. "Believe us," they say, "there's nothing we'd rather do than come up with a pill that messes with our hormones, so we can take this burden from the women, who have been unfairly forced to bear it for far too long. In fact, we'd probably finish developing the male birth-control pill tonight, but we have to play league softball."

A TYPICAL IUD

How Much Does It Cost to Have a Baby?

In primitive times, having a baby was very inexpensive. When women were ready to give birth, they simply went off and squat-

PRIMITIVE BIRTHING

charge you much more. It is a good idea to "shop around" before you settle on a doctor. Ask about the condition of his Mercedes. Ask about the competence of his mechanic. Don't be shy! After all, you're paying for it.

ted in a field; this cost nothing except for a nominal field-rental charge. Today, of course, the medical profession prefers that you have your baby in a hospital, because only there can doctors, thanks to the many advances in medical equipment and techniques, receive large sums of money.

It is difficult to predict exactly what the doctor's bill for your pregnancy will be, because every situation is different. If your doctor's Mercedes-Benz is running well, he may charge you as little as $2,000; if there are complications, such as that he has been hearing a little ticking sound in the transmission lately, then he may be forced to

The Cost of Everything after the Baby Is Born Right Up until It Goes to College or, God Help You, Graduate School

Again, it is very hard to be specific here, largely because I haven't done any research. In my own case, I estimate that the cost of raising our son, Robert, to age three, which is where he is at the moment, breaks down as follows:

> Little metal cars—$13,000
> Everything else—$4,000

If we extrapolate this out for the next 18 years, assuming that inflation continues, and that we don't have a nuclear war, which would pretty much render the point moot, we can conclude that in the long term a child can cost just scads of money. Maybe you should go back and read the section on birth control.

Should the Woman Quit Her Job to Have a Baby?

The advantage of quitting your job is that if you want to, you can make a really nasty speech to your boss, right in front of everybody, where you tell him he's incompetent and has the worst case of bodily odor in the annals of medicine. The disadvantage is that you'll lose your income, which means for the next eight or nine years the only new article of clothing you will be able to afford for yourself will be dress shields.

The advantage of keeping your job is that you will be able to stand around the Xerox machine for a couple of months showing pictures of your child to your co-workers, who will ooh and ahh even though very young infants tend to look like unwashed fruit.

What about Insurance?

Don't worry. Your insurance needs will automatically be taken care of by squadrons of insurance salesmen, who can detect a pregnant woman up to 11 miles away on a calm day, and who will show up at your house carrying sleeping bags and enough freeze-dried food to enable them to stay for weeks if necessary.

The Intangible Benefits

Of course, you can't reduce children to mere dollars and cents. There are many intangible benefits, by which I mean benefits that, when coupled with 50 cents, will buy you a cup of coffee.

For example, I know a person named Michael who, although he does not personally own any children, once got a major benefit from his five-year-old nephew. What happened was they were at this big open-air concert in Boston to celebrate the Bicentennial, and when it was over the crowd was enormous and it looked as though they'd never get out. So Michael held his nephew aloft and yelled, "Sick child! Sick child! Make way!" loud enough so nobody could hear the nephew saying, "I'm not sick, Uncle Mike." And the crowd made way, which meant Mike got home hours sooner than he would have otherwise.

So there is an example of a person getting a large intangible benefit from a child, and it wasn't even technically his child. Also, you can get terrific tax deductions for children. Of course, the same can be said for insulation, but you'd look like an idiot, waving insulation aloft at an outdoor concert.

Chapter 2

Pregnancy

THE FEMALE REPRODUCTIVE ORGANS

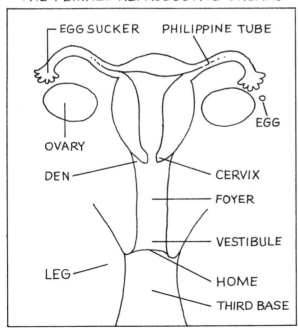

What on earth is going on inside pregnant women that makes them become so large and weepy? This is the fascinating biological topic we will explore in this chapter, at least until we start to feel nauseous.

The Female Reproductive System

The female reproductive system is extremely complicated, because females contain a great many organs, with new ones being discovered every day. Connecting these organs is an elaborate network of over seven statute miles of tubes and canals (see diagram). Nobody really understands this system. Burly male doctors called "gynecologists" are always groping around in there with rubber gloves, trying to figure out what's going on. Or so they claim.

Fertilization

The fertilization process starts in the ovaries, which each month produce an egg. After a hearty breakfast, this egg treks down the fallopian tubes, where it is propositioned by millions of sperm, which are extremely small, totally insincere one-celled animals. Often, to attract the egg, the sperm will engage in ritual behavior, such as ruf-

---

The Stages of Development of the Fetus

WEEK 5:   The fetus is only 6.7 liters in circumference yet has already developed the ability to shriek in airplanes.

WEEK 10:   The fetus is almost 12 milli-pedes in longitude and has a prehensile tail and wings. It will probably lose these things before it is born.

WEEK 20:   The fetus measures 4 on the Richter scale and is perusing mail-order catalogs from the Fisher-Price company.

WEEKS 30–40:   The fetus is on vacation.

WEEK 50:   The fetus can run the 100-meter dash in 10.23 seconds and has devel-oped an interest in pottery.

---

fling their neck feathers. No wait, I'm think-ing of birds.

Anyway, the egg, a fat and globular kind of cell with very little self-esteem, finds itself in this dimly lit fallopian tube sur-rounded by all these sleek, well-traveled sperm, and sooner or later one of them manages to penetrate. Then the sperm all saunter off, winking and nudging each other toward the bile duct, while the fertilized egg slinks down to the uterus, an organ shaped like Webster Groves, Missouri. The egg attaches itself to the uterine wall, and thus begins an incredibly subtle and complex chain of hormonal secretions that signal to the woman's body that it is time to start shopping around for fluffy little baby gar-ments. Pregnancy has begun.

Pregnancy and Diet

You must remember that when you are pregnant, you are eating for two. But you must also remember that the other one of you is about the size of a golf ball, so let's not go overboard with it. I mean, a lot of preg-nant women eat as though the other person they're eating for is Orson Welles. The instant they find out they're pregnant they rush right out and buy a case of Mallomars, and within days they've expanded to the size of barrage balloons.

Answers to Common Questions about Pregnancy

Q. WHAT WILL HAPPEN TO MY BODY DURING PREGNANCY BE- SIDES THAT I WILL BECOME HUGE AND TIRED AND THROW UP A LOT AND BE CONSTIPATED AND DE- VELOP HEMORRHOIDS AND HAVE TO URINATE ALL THE TIME AND HAVE LEG CRAMPS AND VARICOSE VEINS?

A. Many women also have lower back pain.

Q. IS IT SAFE TO GAMBLE AND CURSE DURING PREGNANCY?

A. Yes, but during the first trimester you should avoid gaudy jewelry.

Q. HOW LONG WILL I BE PREG- NANT?

A. Most of us learn in health class that the human gestation period is nine months. Like most things we learn in health class, this is a lie. The only people who still believe it are doctors, who make a big fuss out of giving you a "due date" nine months from when they think you were fertilized, as if it takes some kind of elabo- rate medical training to operate a calen- dar.

I have done exhaustive research on this question in the form of talking to my friends and listening in on other people's conversations in the supermarket checkout line, and I have concluded that no woman has ever given birth on her "due date." About a quarter of all pregnant women give birth "prematurely," which means during the doctor's vacation that immediately pre- cedes the "due date." All other women— and ask them if you don't believe me— remain pregnant for at least 14 months, and sometimes much longer if the weather has been unusually hot.

Q. CAN I HAVE SEX WITH MY HUSBAND WHILE I'M PREGNANT?

A. No.

Q. WELL, CAN I HAVE SEX WITH SOMEONE ELSE'S HUSBAND?

A. I don't see why not.

Keep in mind that it's a *baby* you're eating for. If you're going to eat for it, don't eat like an adult; eat like a *baby*. This doesn't mean you can't have Mallomars; it means you must hold them in your hands until the chocolate melts and then rub it into your hair and the sofa. If you eat at a restaurant, feel free to order that steak you crave, but have the waiter cut it into 650,000 tiny pieces and then refuse to touch them, preferring instead to chew and swallow the cocktail napkin and then throw up a little bit on your dress.

Important Advice for Husbands

The key here is to be sensitive. You must not let your wife think you find her unattractive just because she's getting tremendously fat. Go out of you way to reassure her on this point. From time to time, say to her: "I certainly don't find you unattractive just because you're getting tremendously fat." If you go to a party where every woman in the room is slinky and lithe except your wife, who is wearing a maternity outfit that makes her look like a convertible sofa, be sure to remark from time to time, in a strident voice, that you can't judge a book by its cover. Your wife is bound to remember this sensitive gesture.

During her pregnancy your wife will have many emotional moods caused by the fact that there are gallons of hormones racing around inside her. The two of you will be sitting in your living room, watching the evening news on television, when all of a sudden she'll run into the bedroom in tears because of a report about a monsoon wiping out a distant Asian village. Follow her. Comfort her. Tell her: "They're just distant Asians, for God's sake."

Teaching Your Child in the Uterus

Can you teach your child while it's still in the uterus? The answer is yes, at least according to this couple I saw on the "Phil Donahue Show" once, and I don't see why they would lie about it. Their kids all came out of the womb with a deep appreciation for classical music. Frankly, I don't understand why parents think this is so important, because as I recall my youth, children who appreciated classical music were infinitely more likely to get beat up on the playground. The smart move, if you want your child to have the respect and admiration of its peers, would be to teach it how to spit convincingly or lead cheers.

But never mind what you teach the child while it's in the uterus; the important thing

FETAL POSITIONS

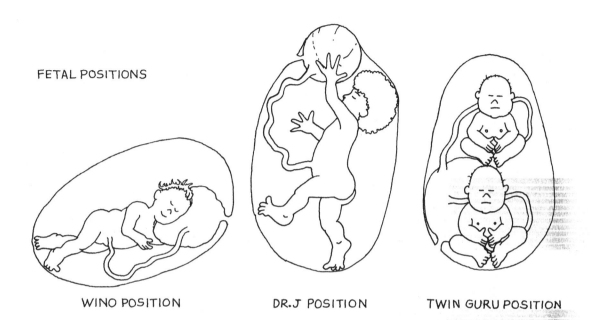

WINO POSITION   DR. J POSITION   TWIN GURU POSITION

is that you *can* teach it, and you'd better, if you want it to get into Harvard Medical School. Of course, the teaching method has to be very simple. I mean, you can't go in there with slide projectors or anything. Where would you plug them in? So you'll pretty much have to content yourself with yelling at the stomach. This is the man's job, because let's face it, the woman would look pretty stupid yelling at her own stomach.

So whenever the two of you have a spare moment together, such as when you're waiting to cash a check at the bank, the man should lean over and yell, in the general direction of the woman's uterus, something

like "THE CAPITAL OF NORTH DAKOTA IS PIERRE." Or maybe that's South Dakota. I can never keep the state capitals straight, because when I was in the uterus, back in 1946, Phil Donahue hadn't been invented yet.

The Baby Shower

Probably the single most grueling ordeal a woman must endure during pregnancy is the baby shower. What happens is you have to sit in the middle of a group of women and repeatedly open gifts, and every time you

THE BABY SHOWER

open one, you have to adopt a delighted expression, then hold the gift up—even if it is disposable diapers—and exclaim, "Oh! How cute!" In some cases this goes on for hours, and all you are permitted to eat is tiny sandwiches with the crusts cut off.

At one time, most women relied on drugs to get through their showers. But more and more, women are practicing "natural" shower techniques, which allow them, through careful preparation, to have perfectly safe showers without the use of artificial substances.

The key is teamwork between you and your husband. Well in advance of the expected shower date, the two of you should practice regularly at home. Sit on the sofa while your husband hands you various objects, and practice holding them up and exclaiming, "Oh! How cute!" You must practice this every night until no matter what he hands you—an ashtray, a snow tire, a reptile, etc.—you can still appear to be genuinely delighted.

Chapter 3

Getting Ready for Baby

Safety Precautions around the Home

Babies are equipped at birth with a number of instinctive reflexes and behavior patterns that cause them to spend their first several years trying to kill themselves. If your home contains a sharp, toxic object, your baby will locate it; if your home contains no such object, your baby will try to obtain one via mail order. Therefore, you must comb through your house or apartment and eliminate all unsafe things, including:

dirt	forks	old copies of
germs	spittoons	*Penthouse*
attics	stairs	magazine
stoves	water	

You should also be sure to have the electrical system taken‚out. You cannot "child-proof" it by plugging those little plastic caps into all the outlets. Children emerge from the womb knowing how to remove those caps by means of an instinctive outlet-cap-plucking reflex that doctors regard as one of the key indicators that the child is normal.

Baby's Room

Baby's room must be kept at a steady temperature of 72 degrees Fahrenheit and a relative humidity of 63 percent, and it must have wallpaper with clowns holding blue, red, and green balloons. Baby's room should be close enough to your room so that you can hear baby cry, unless you want to get some sleep, in which case baby's room should be in Peru.

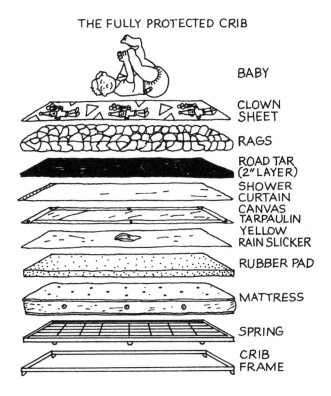

THE FULLY PROTECTED CRIB

BABY

CLOWN SHEET

RAGS

ROAD TAR (2" LAYER)

SHOWER CURTAIN

CANVAS TARPAULIN

YELLOW RAIN SLICKER

RUBBER PAD

MATTRESS

SPRING

CRIB FRAME

Baby's Crib

The important thing to remember here is that baby does not sleep in the crib. Baby sleeps in the car. Baby uses the crib as a place to cry and go to the bathroom, so the crib has to be fully protected. To make up the crib, first put down the mattress, then a rubber pad, then a yellow rain slicker, then a stout canvas tarpaulin, then a shower curtain, then a two-inch-thick layer of road tar, then a bale of highly absorbent rags, then a cute little sheet with pictures of clowns holding blue, red, and green balloons. You should have lots of spares of all these things.

Other Furniture for Baby's Room

Your best bet is an industrial dumpster.

Baby's Clothes

Have you ever stopped to ask yourself why so few high-level corporate executives are babies? The reason is that most babies do not dress for success.

Next time you're in a shopping mall, take a look at what these unsuccessful babies are wearing. Somewhere on virtually every

AN EXTENDED-WEAR DIAPER

A TYPICAL MALL-BABY

child's outfit will be embroidered either a barnyard animal or a cretin statement such as "Lil' Angel." Many of the babies will be wearing bib overalls, despite overwhelming scientific evidence that such garments reduce the wearer's apparent I.Q. by as many as 65 points. Some of the girl babies will be wearing tights and petticoats that stick straight out horizontally in such a way as to reveal an enormous unsightly diaper bulge, causing them to look like miniature ballerinas with bladder disorders. Really young babies will be encased in fluffy pastel zip-up sacks with no place for the poop to get out, so that after a few hours in the mall they are no more than little pastel sacks of poop with babies' heads sticking out.

You look at these babies, and you realize that they will never be considered for responsible positions until they learn to dress more sensibly. So when you're shopping for clothes for your baby, stick to the time-tested dress-for-success classics—your pinstripes, your lightweight wool suits in blue or gray, stout brogans, etc. And don't neglect the accessories! A baby sucking on a cheap pink plastic rattle is likely to be passed over at promotion time in favor of a baby sucking on a leather rattle with brass fittings.

Baby's Toys

Your friends and relatives will buy your baby lots and lots of cute dolls and stuffed animals, all of which you should throw in the trash compactor immediately. Sure, they look cute to you, but to the baby they appear to be the size of station wagons. So all night long, while you're safe in your animal-free bedroom, your baby is lying there, surrounded by these gigantic creatures. Try to imagine sleeping with an eight-foot-high Raggedy Ann sitting just inches away, staring at you! Especially if you had no way of knowing whether Raggedy Anns were vicious! No wonder babies cry so much at night!

So you don't want cute creatures with eyes. You also don't want so-called educational toys that claim to teach "spatial relationships," because the only spatial relationship newborn babies care about is whether they can fit things into their mouths. This means you want toys that will fit safely and comfortably in a baby's mouth. The best way to select such toys is to try them out in your own mouth, bearing in mind that yours has eight times the volume of baby's. When you go to the toy store, ask to see eight of each potential toy; if you can stuff them all comfortably in your mouth, you should buy one. Remind the salesclerk to sterilize the other seven, so as not to pass infectious diseases on to the next shopper. The clerk will appreciate this thoughtful reminder.

In a later chapter, I'll talk about buying toys for you child when it has acquired the conceptual and manipulative skills necessary to break things.

THE "NO" TOYS

THE "YES" TOYS

Diapers: Cloth vs. Disposable

At one time, back during the Korean War, most people rejected disposable diapers because they preferred the natural soft feel of cloth. Then it finally began to dawn on people that the natural soft feel of cloth begins to lose some of its charm when it has been pooped and peed on repeatedly.

So now everybody uses disposable diapers. Oh, I realize there are diaper services that come to your house and drop off clean cloth diapers and pick up the dirty ones, but even those diapers are now disposable. The instant the driver is out of sight of your house, he hurls the dirty diapers into the street and drives off briskly.

The only problem with disposable diapers is that they are starting to overflow the world's refuse-disposal facilities; scientists now predict that if the present trend continues, by the year 1997 the entire planet will smell like the men's room in a bar frequented by motorcycle gangs. But this is not really as serious as it sounds, because scientists also believe that several years before 1997 the polar ice caps are going to melt. Also, we could always have a nuclear war. So I would definitely go with the disposable diapers.

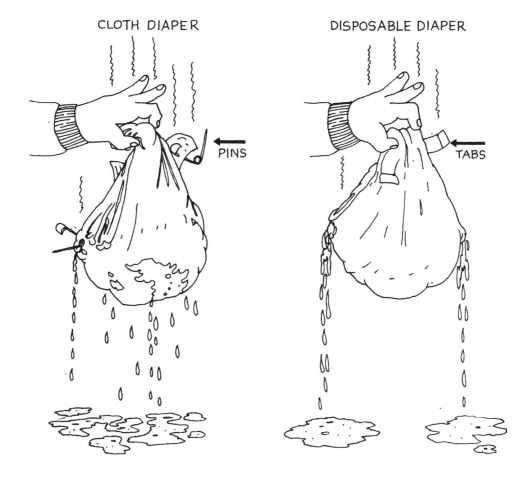

CLOTH DIAPER

DISPOSABLE DIAPER

← PINS

← TABS

Chapter 4

Preparing for Birth

An Important Message about Professional Childbirth-Preparation Terminology

Before you have your baby, you're going to be dealing with a number of professional childbirth experts, so you ought to know that they all have this very strict rule: when they talk about childbirth, they never use the word "pain." Granted, this is like talking about the Pacific Ocean without using the word "water," but the way they see it, if they were to tell you women, in clear language, what is really involved in getting this largish object out of your body, none of you would have babies, and the professional childbirth experts would have to find another source of income.

So they use the International Childbirth Professional Code Word for pain, which is "contraction." To the nonexpert, a "contraction" sounds like, at worst, maybe a mild muscle cramp, but it actually describes a sensation similar to that of having professional football players smash their fists into your uterine wall. In a "strong contraction," the players are also wearing skis.

It's quite natural for you to be apprehensive about the pain of childbirth. I was terrified of it myself, until I did a little research and learned there was no way I would ever have to go through it. So let's take a thorough, informed, scientific look at this much-misunderstood topic, and maybe we can clear up your concerns, although I doubt it.

Here are two actual diagrams, drawn with the aid of modern medical expertise, showing the insides of a woman just before and just after giving birth:

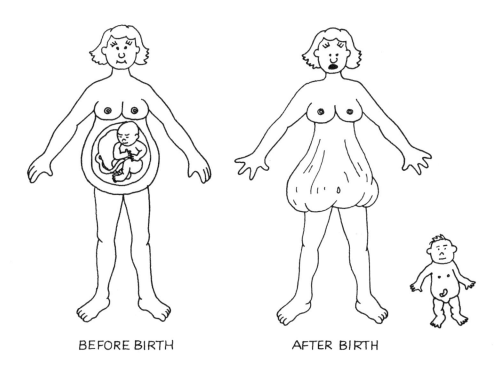

BEFORE BIRTH   AFTER BIRTH

What these diagrams reveal to those of us trained to understand them is that there is an entire baby inside the pregnant woman, and somehow during childbirth it comes out. This is the part that stumps us, because despite all of our modern medical expertise, we frankly cannot see how such a thing is possible. All we really know about it is that it seems to hurt like crazy.

If you'd like more technical details on the childbirth process, I suggest you view one of the many fine prairie dramas on television wherein some pathetic wispy-haired pioneer woman goes into labor during a blizzard in the most god-awful desolate prairie place, such as Kansas. Nothing brings on labor like a prairie blizzard. Women have been known to give birth in prairie blizzards even when they weren't actually pregnant.

Anyway, on these prairie dramas the pioneer woman lies around moaning and writhing, which should give you an idea of what childbirth is like, except that on television it takes about as long as an episode of "Little House on the Prairie," whereas in real life it can take as long as "Roots."

But don't worry, because later in this chapter we'll talk about a wonderful new modern natural technique for coping with contractions. I won't describe this amazing technique right away, because I don't want you to find out yet that it's really just deep breathing.

How Your Mother Had Babies, and Why We Now Feel It Was All Wrong

Here is the system that was used for having babies during the Eisenhower Administration: At the first sign of pregnancy, the husband would rush the wife to the hospital, where she would be given modern medical drugs that would keep her from

GROWN-UP DRUG-DAMAGED BABIES OF (LEFT TO RIGHT) THE 40s, 50s, AND 60s

feeling contractions or anything else, including a volcanic eruption in the delivery room. This way the woman felt very little pain. Often she didn't regain consciousness until her child was entering the fourth grade.

One big problem with this system was that drugs can have adverse effects on the baby, as is evidenced by the fact that every single person born during the 40s, 50s, or 60s is really screwed up. Another problem was that the father had very little to do with the birth. His job was to sit in the waiting room with the other fathers and smoke cigarettes and read old copies of *Field and Stream* and wonder what the hell was taking so long. When the baby was born, the nurses would clean it up as best as they could and show it to the father, then he'd go home to bumble around and have humorous kitchen episodes until his wife got back on her feet and could resume cooking. This system deprived the husband of the chance to witness the glorious moment when his child came into the world, not to mention all the other various solids and fluids that come into the world with the child.

So today we have a much better childbirth system. Federal law now requires the man to watch the woman have the baby, and the woman is not allowed to have any drugs unless she agrees, in writing, to feel guilty. In some ways, we're back to the old prairie method of baby-having, only we do it in modern hospitals, so the husband doesn't have to boil water. All the water-boiling is now done by trained health-care professionals for about $65 a gallon.

Choosing a Hospital

The most important thing to remember in choosing a hospital is that there must be no Dairy Queen between it and you. Medical science has been unable to develop a way to get a pregnant woman, even in the throes of labor, past a Dairy Queen without stopping for a chocolate milk shake. This could waste precious time on the way to the hospital. Even worse, the woman could start having the baby right there in the Dairy Queen, with nobody to help her except her husband and various teenage Dairy Queen employees all smeared with butterscotch and wearing those idiot hats.

Also, you should pick a hospital you feel comfortable in. Most people feel uneasy about hospitals, possibly because the instant you walk through the door medical personnel grab you and remove your blood and stick tubes up your nose. But in deciding where you're going to have your baby, you must overcome these fears. You must barge right into the hospital and ask questions. If you have no questions, use these:

1. How much does this hospital weigh?
2. What's that funny smell?

Don't leave until you get the answers!

Childbirth Classes: Learning to Breathe

Before you can have your baby, you have to attend childbirth classes wherein you openly discuss the sexual organs with people you barely know. You get used to it. You'll get so that when your instructor passes around a life-size plastic replica of the cervix, you'll all hold it up and make admiring comments, as if it were a prize floral arrangement. You'll get to know the uterus so well that you'd recognize one anywhere. Also, you'll see actual color movies of babies being born, so that you'll be prepared for the fact that they come out looking like Mister Potato Head.

But the main thing you'll do in childbirth classes is learn the amazing new modern natural technique for getting through contractions, namely deep breathing. Now I will admit that when our instructor first talked about getting through labor with nothing but deep breathing, my immediate impulse was to rush out and buy three or four quarts

THE CERVIX

of morphine, just in case. But after several weeks of practicing the breathing techniques, my wife and I became convinced that, by golly, they really worked! Obviously we were hyperventilating.

The key to the technique is to breathe in a different way for each stage of labor, as is illustrated by the accompanying simple chart.

The Magic Word

One last thing. In childbirth classes, you will be taught, with much ceremony, a Se-

Correct Way to Breathe during Labor		
NAME OF LABOR STAGE	SYMP- TOMS	CORRECT BREATHING TECHNIQUE
Early	Pain	Inhale for 11 sec.; exhale through teeth in six sharp, 2-second gasps, forming mouth as if to say "carnivorous"
Orientation	Pain	Inhale for 55 sec.; exhale towards Mecca with mouth formed in shape of a lowercase "r"
Transmission	Pain	Inhale for 3 sec.; exhale gradually for 107 sec. through partner's teeth; hum "Turkey in the Straw" (but NOT the chorus)
Baby Coming Out	Really awful pain	Do not inhale; exhale for 25–30 min. with mouth formed as if to shriek

cret Magical Anti-Contraction Word that the woman is supposed to say when things get really awful, when the professional football players in her uterus are wearing skis *and* carrying sharpened poles. Technically, this word is supposed to be revealed only in childbirth classes, but I have decided to print it below for use in case of emergency.

WARNING: THE NEXT PARAGRAPH CONTAINS THE SECRET MAGICAL ANTI-CONTRACTION WORD. DO NOT READ THIS PARAGRAPH UNLESS YOU ARE SINCERELY IN THE PROCESS OF HAVING A BABY.

The word is "hout." Rhymes with "trout." It may not look like much, but it has been scientifically shown to be over twice as effective against contractions as the next leading word, "Ohmigod." You may hear another secret word in your childbirth classes, but "hout" did it for us. Our instructor had us practice it for hours in class—you have to get the tip of your tongue right on the edge of your front teeth—and it really helped my wife get through those first few contractions. After that, she switched over to "AAAAAAAARRRRRRGGGUUU-NNNNH," which is not an officially approved word, but seemed to work well for her.

Chapter 5

The Actual Blessed Event

Childbirth is like vampires: it never strikes before sundown. If you feel something that seems like contractions during the day, you're actually having what is called "false labor." Sometimes false labor can be very realistic, in which case you may have to go to the hospital, where you will be examined by a false doctor, who may even deliver an anatomically correct doll.

But real labor always begins at 3:15 A.M. eastern standard time, because that is when every obstetrician in the country is in deepest sleep. As soon as the contractions start, you should call your obstetrician, who will answer the phone and, without even waking up, say: "How far apart are the contractions?" You can give any answer you want ("About two feet," for example), and then the obstetrician will say, "You'd better come on in to the hospital." Then he'll roll over onto his side, still completely unconscious, and resume snoring.

At this time, you should gather up the things you'll need in the hospital (don't forget your passport!) and set off. Husbands, here is how you should drive: Sit on the edge of the driver's seat with your face one inch from the windshield and grip the steering wheel so firmly that little pieces of it keep breaking off in your hands. Every eight or nine seconds, jerk your head down violently to look at the gas gauge, then give your wife's knee a firm clench for one-tenth of a second and grimace at her and say,

CORRECT DRIVING POSITION

"Everything's going to be fine." But despite this reassuring exterior, husbands, you must be alert and prepared for any problem that could prevent you from getting to the hospital in time.

What to Do If You Can't Get to the Hospital

At all costs, you must not panic. Stay calm. A good way to do this is to play word games, such as the one where you start with a letter, and then the other person adds a letter, and so on, the idea being that you are spelling an actual word, but you don't want to supply the last letter. For extra fun, you can say that the loser has to get out and run around the car backwards three times at a red light. Besides livening up the game, this will attract the attention of the police, who might help deliver your baby in a gruff but kindly manner, the way they do in anecdotes from *Reader's Digest*. Or they might beat you with clubs.

What Will Happen to You If You Get to the Hospital

At the maternity ward, you will be greeted by kindly nurses who will do a number of unspeakably degrading things to you while the hospital operator tries to wake up your obstetrician. Then you will be placed in a little room where your husband can sit with his little clipboard and stopwatch and time your contractions, just like you learned in childbirth class, until you swat his goddamn clipboard and stopwatch across the room and demand to be killed, which is the sign that you have gone from "contractions" to "strong contractions."

Three Problems That Could Prevent You from Getting to the Hospital in Time

1. Your car radio could explode for no apparent reason.

2. You could be stopped by police who are looking for escaped radicals, and who think your wife's stomach is a bomb and call in the Explosives Disposal Unit to cover her with sand.

3. You could get stuck behind a member of the Elderly People with Enormous Cars Club, driving smack dab in the middle of the road at two miles an hour in search of an all-night drugstore to buy new batteries for his hearing aid, so he can't hear you honk.

At this time, you will be taken to the delivery room, where you will be placed in the Standard Childbirth Position, illustrated below. Medical researchers have tried for decades to come up with a childbirth position even more humiliating than this one, but they have had no success. Two of the alternative childbirth positions are diagramed on the following page.

STANDARD CHILDBIRTH POSITION

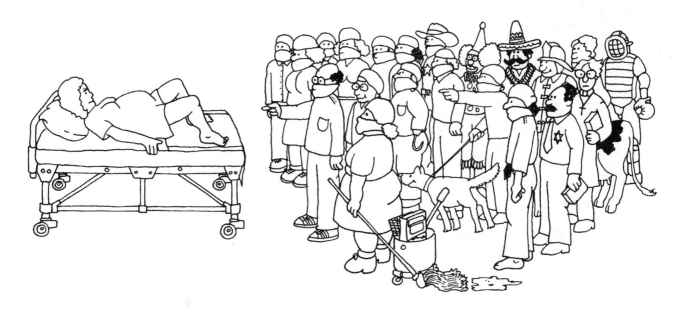

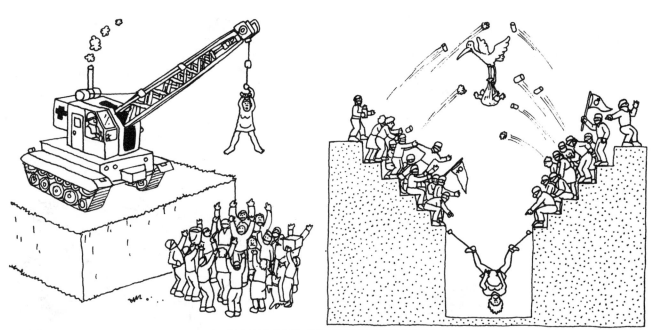

ALTERNATIVE CHILDBIRTH POSITIONS

While you're in this delicate position in the delivery room, you may be a bit embarrassed, especially since there are people standing around wearing masks and watching you. So let me explain who these people are. You have your obstetrician, of course, unless the hospital operator has been unable to rouse him, in which case he will actually be a life-size obstetrician puppet operated from behind by a nurse trained to mimic obstetricians' voices. You also have your husband, assuming he has been able to wash away the little crumbled bits of steering wheel embedded in his hands.

Then you have your pediatrician, and an anesthesiologist to stand by in case the doctors decide that the delivery is not costing enough. Also you have at least one nurse to assist each of these doctors; you have three medical students; you have one law student;

and you have Billy Ray Johnson, who is actually a retired beet farmer who just happens to like hanging around delivery rooms and watch people have babies.

So that's it, just 12 of you, unless Billy Ray has brought friends to share this wondrous moment.

The Big Moment

And what is it like? That, of course, is what you want to know: What is it *really* like?

I don't have the vaguest idea, of course. But I do remember what it sounded like when my wife had our son. I was at one end of my wife, shouting words of encouragement to her head, the doctor and nurse were shouting to the other end of her body. It sounded like a group of extremely sincere people trying to help an elephant dislodge a Volkswagen from its throat:

DOCTOR: You're doing just great, Beth! Just great! Really! Isn't she doing great?
NURSE: She sure is! She's doing just great!
ME: You're really doing great, honey! Really!
BETH: AAAAAAAAAAAAARRRRRRRR RRRRRRRUUUUNNNNNNNNNNNNN NNNGGGGGGGGGGGGGGGGGGGGGG GHHHHHHHHHHH.
DOCTOR: That was just great! Really!

And so on, for quite a while, until finally Robert came out, and immediately demanded to be put back in. My wife and I were very happy. I remember hugging her head.

What to Do Immediately after Birth

Close your eyes tightly. This is in case the doctor takes it into his head to show you the placenta, which is a highly unattractive object that comes out close on the heels of the baby. In the old days, when people were decent, the placenta was disposed of quickly and quietly and was never talked about in polite society. But now people bandy it about openly in public, as if it were a prize-winning bass.

Bonding

While the obstetrician is finishing up, the pediatrician will wrap your baby in a blanket and hand it to you so that you can marvel at the miracle of birth and everything. My only warning here is that you should not hold your baby too long, or you will become "bonded" to it and have to be tugged apart by burly hospital aides.

Chapter 6

The Hospital Stay

A Reassuring Word for First-Time Parents about Hospital Baby-Identification Procedures

A common fear among new parents is that, as a result of a mix-up in the nursery, some kind of terrible mistake will be made, such as that they'll wind up taking home Yasser Arafat's baby. This fear is groundless. When a baby is born, a hospital person immediately puts a little plastic tag around its wrist with the words "NOT YASSER ARAFAT'S BABY" printed on it in indelible ink. So whichever baby you wind up with, you can be sure it isn't his.

Visitors in the Hospital

Maternity ward visitors are an excellent source of amusement, because they always feel obligated to say flattering things about newborn babies, which of course look like enormous fruit fly larvae. One fun trick is to show your visitors somebody else's baby. "She definitely has your eyes!" your visitors will exclaim. For real entertainment, have the nurse bring you a live ferret, wrapped in a baby blanket. "She's very alert!" your visitors will remark, as the ferret lacerates their fingers with needle-sharp teeth.

How Long Should the Mother Stay in the Hospital after the Baby Comes Out?

As long as possible. For one thing, as long as you're in the hospital you can wear a bathrobe all day. This means you won't have to face up to the fact that even after expelling the baby and all the baby-related fluids and solids, you still have hips the size of vending machines from all the Mallomars you ate back when you thought you were going to be pregnant forever.

For another thing, the hospital employs trained professional personnel to change the baby's diapers, etc., so all you have to do is lounge around in your bathrobe looking serene and complaining about the food. If you go home, you'll have to take care of the baby *and* confront the fact that you did not once clean behind any of the toilets during the last four months of your pregnancy because you couldn't bend over.

The hospital personnel will try to make you leave after a couple of days, but all you have to do is waddle off to another room and plop down on the bed. There are so many comings and goings in a maternity ward that it will be several days before they catch on to you and try to make you leave again, at which time you can just waddle off to another room. You can probably keep this up until your baby starts to walk unassisted from the nursery to your room at feeding time.

Naming Your Baby

A good way to pass the time while you're in the hospital is to argue loudly with your husband about what to name the baby. You should get started on this as soon as possible, because both of you are likely to have strong views. For example, he may want to name the baby "John," after a favorite uncle, while you may hate "John" because it reminds you of a former boyfriend, not to mention that the baby is a girl.

There are some names new parents should avoid altogether. You shouldn't name a boy "Cyril" or "Percy," because the other boys will want to punch him repeatedly in the mouth, and I can't say as I blame them. And you shouldn't give a girl's name a cute spelling, such as "Cyndi," because no matter how many postgraduate degrees she gets she will never advance any further than clerk-typist.

In recent years, it has become fashionable to give children extremely British-sounding names, such as "Jessica." I think this is an excellent idea. Despite the fact that Great Britain has been unable to produce a car that can be driven all the way across a shopping mall parking lot without major engine failure, Americans think that any-

ATYPICAL CYRIL   A TYPICAL PERCY

thing British is really terrific. So I recommend you give your baby the most British name you can think up, such as "Queen Elizabeth" or "Big Ben" or "Crumpet Scone-Hayes."

Some Heavy Thoughts to Think during the Hospital Stay

The hospital stay is a good time for you, as new parents, to share some quiet moments together listening to the woman on the other side of the curtain discuss her bowel movements with her mother via telephone. This is also a time for you to marvel at your baby's incredibly small feet and hands and to reflect on the fact that this is a real human life, a life that you have created, just the two of you; a tiny, helpless life that you are completely responsible for. Makes you want to hop right on a plane for the Azores, doesn't it? I mean, what do the two of you know about being responsible for a human life? The two of you can't even consistently locate clean underwear, for God's sake!

Mother Nature understands this. That is why she has constructed babies so that even the most profoundly incompetent person, even a person who takes astrology seriously and writes angry, semiliterate letters to the television station when it changes the time at which it broadcasts "Family Feud," can raise babies successfully. All a newborn baby really needs is food, warmth, and love, pretty much like a hamster, only with fewer signs of intelligence.

So don't worry; you'll do fine. Some day, when your child has grown into a teenager and gotten drunk and crashed your new car into the lobby of the home for the aged during the annual Christmas party, you'll look back on the hamster era and laugh about how worried you were.

In the next chapter, we'll talk about how laughably easy it is to take care of a newborn baby, provided you don't do anything else.

Chapter 7

Maintenance of a New Baby

Finally will come the big day when the hospital authorities order the wife to leave, and the two of you take your new baby home. There is nothing quite like the moment when a young couple leaves the hospital, walking with that characteristic new-parent gait that indicates an obsessive fear of dropping the baby on its head. Finally! It's just the three of you, on your own!

This independence will last until you get maybe eight feet from the hospital door, where you'll be assaulted by grandmothers offering advice. The United States Constitution empowers grandmothers to stop any young person on the street with a baby and offer advice, and they take this responsibility very seriously. If they see your baby without a little woolen hat, they will advise you that your baby is too cold. If your baby has a hat, they will advise you that your baby is too warm. Always they will offer this advice in a tone of voice that makes it clear they do not expect your baby to survive the afternoon in the care of such incompetents as yourselves.

The best way to handle advice from random grandmothers is to tell them that you appreciate their concern, but that you feel it is your responsibility to make your own decisions about your child's welfare. If that doesn't work, try driving them off with sticks. Otherwise, they'll follow you home and hang around under your windows.

Now let's talk about maintaining your new baby.

The Basic Baby Mood Cycle

This is the Basic Baby Mood Cycle, which all babies settle into once they get over being born:

MOOD ONE: Just about to cry
MOOD TWO: Crying
MOOD THREE: Just finished crying

MOOD ONE

MOOD TWO

MOOD THREE

Your major job is to keep your baby in Mood Three as much as possible. Here is the traditional way to do this. When the baby starts to cry, the two of you should pass it back and forth repeatedly and recite these words in unison: "Do you suppose he's hungry? He can't be hungry. He just ate. Maybe he needs to be burped. No, that's not it. Maybe his diaper needs to be changed. No, it's dry. What could be wrong? Do you think maybe he's hungry?" And so on, until the baby can't stand it any more and decides to go to sleep.

When your baby is awake and not crying, it will follow specific air molecules around the room with its eyes. For years, scientists thought the reason newborn babies waved their eyes around in such seemingly random ways was that they couldn't really focus on anything, but we now know that, thanks to the fact that they have such small eyes, they can actually see molecules whooshing around, which is a much more interesting thing to watch than a bunch of parents and relatives waving stupid rattles in their faces.

Also, babies receive signals from outer space, bringing messages from other galaxies that only babies can detect. These messages cause the baby to smile (if the message is a joke) or look startled (if it is bad news, such as the explosion of a popular star).

When Should You Feed Your Baby?

During the day, you should feed your baby just before the phone rings. At night, you should feed your baby immediately after you have fallen asleep. After each feeding, you should pat your baby gently on the back until it pukes on your shoulder.

BABY THROWING UP IN CHURCH

Should You Breast-Feed or Bottle-Feed Your Baby?

I'm surprised you even have to ask. All of us modern childbirth experts feel very

BABY'S VIEW OF A BREAST AND A BOTTLE

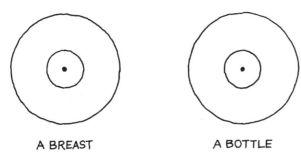

A BREAST   A BOTTLE

strongly that you should breast-feed your child. There are two major reasons:

1. Your mother *didn't* breast-feed, and as I pointed out in the chapter on childbirth, we now know that everything your mother did was wrong.

2. Breast-feeding is better for the baby. Much has been written on this subject, reams and reams of information in hundreds of excellent books and articles which I frankly have been unable to read because I would never get this book finished on time. But the basic idea, as I understand it, is that *bottle* milk is designed primarily for baby *cows,* whereas your baby is not a cow at all! It can't even stand up! Am I getting too technical here?

Anyway, all your really smart, with-it trendsetters are into breast-feeding today. Go into any swank New York City night spot and you'll see dozens of chic women such as Leona Helmsley breast-feeding, many of them with rented babies.

Learning to Breast-Feed

Like many new mothers, you may feel ashamed that you don't just automatically know how to breast-feed. You know there must be more to it than just shoving the breast into the baby's mouth, because otherwise people wouldn't keep writing enormous books about it. But just what *are* you sup-

posed to do? You look at pictures in *National Geographic* of women in some primitive South American jungle tribe, women who have never even seen Tupperware, casually breast-feeding their infants, and you think: "How come *they* know how to do it and I don't? What's *wrong* with me?"

Don't be so hard on yourself. Those primitive women have undergone hours and hours of intensive breast-feeding instruction at special training centers funded by the United Nations, and only the top graduates are chosen to appear in *National Geographic* photographs. Yes, they have to be taught, too, so don't be the least bit

44

GIVING BABY A BOTTLE

STEP 1: INSERT BOTTLE.

STEP 2: BABY SHOULD SUCK.

STEP 3: IF BABY DOESN'T SUCK,
CHECK BOTTLE. IF BOTTLE
IS OK...

STEP 4: ...TURN BABY
SO THAT END
WITH HEAD IS UP.

45

ashamed to ask a nurse for help. My wife finally had to ask a nurse, who came in and stuck her (my wife's) breast into my son's mouth. Without the nurse's technical know-how, my wife might have stuck her breast into my son's ear or something, and serious nutritional complications could have developed.

Common Problems with Breast-Feeding

Well, for one thing, you're supposed to switch the baby from one side to the other, but usually the baby wants to stay where it is, and babies develop suction that has been measured at upwards of 6,000 pounds per square inch. You can't get them off with crowbars.

Another common problem is milk supply. Babies love to play little pranks wherein one day they drink about six gallons of milk, which causes a mother to produce like crazy, and the next day the baby drinks maybe an ounce and a half. Some mothers have been known to explode from the pressure.

What Is Colic?

Colic is when your baby cries all the time, and people keep telling you how their kid had the colic for 71 straight months. If your baby gets colic, you should take it to the pediatrician so he can say, "There's nothing to worry about," which is of course absolutely true from his perspective, since he lives in a colic-free home many miles from your baby.

"There's nothing to worry about" is a typical example of the kind of easy-for-you-to-say remarks that pediatricians like to make. Another one is, "Take his temperature rectally every hour," an instruction which, if actually followed, would scar both parent and child emotionally for life. If your baby has diaper rash, your pediatrician may say, "Just leave the diaper off for a while." This would be a wonderful idea if the baby would stop shooting wastes out of its various orifices, but of course the baby cannot do this, which is why it is wearing a diaper in the first place. Not that the pediatrician knows about any of this. His baby is tended by domestics from third world nations.

Changing Your Baby's Diapers

First of all, you must understand that as far as your baby is concerned, you never have to change its diapers. There is no creature on earth so content as a baby with a full diaper. Pooping is one of the few useful skills that very small babies have mastered, and they take tremendous pride in it, especially when they have an audience, such as grandparents or the assembled guests at the christening. They'll wrinkle their little faces up into determined frowns, and they'll really *work* at it, with appropriate loudish grunting noises that will at times drown out the clergyman. After all that effort, they want some time to enjoy their achievement, to wriggle and squirm until poop has oozed into every wrinkle and crevice of the cute little $45 designer baby outfit you bought especially for the christening. So when you change your baby's diaper, don't think you're doing your baby any great favor. As far as your baby is concerned, you're taking away the fruits of its labor. "Why don't you get your own poop?" is what newborn babies would say if they could talk, which thank God they can't.

Now let's talk about diaper-changing technique. The problem with most baby books is that when they show you how to change diapers, they use photographs showing a clean changing table in a well-lit room, and a baby that is devoid of any sign of bodily eliminations. Why would *anybody*, except maybe some kind of pervert, want to change such a baby? No, what you need to know is how to change a really filthy baby, and under difficult conditions, such as in bus station rest rooms where even the germs have diseases.

I'd say restaurants pose the biggest dia-

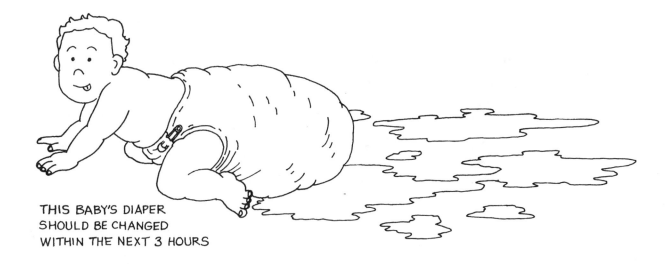

THIS BABY'S DIAPER
SHOULD BE CHANGED
WITHIN THE NEXT 3 HOURS

DINING OUT WITH BABY

per-changing challenge. When my son was three months old, my wife and I took him to a dimly lit, semielegant restaurant, and by the time we examined him closely he had managed to get poop up as far as his *hat*. I mean, we had a major failure of the containment vessel, and there was no sterile little changing table around, just lots of people hoping to dine in a romantic environment. So what you have to do in these situations is go on laughing and chatting as though nothing is wrong, but meanwhile work away like madmen under the table with moist towelettes, which you should buy in freight-car loads.

What I'm saying here is that you need to learn to change diapers furtively, in the dark, and you need to be able to saunter unobtrusively carrying huge wads of reeking towelettes past amorous couples to the rest room trash container, and you do not learn these things in books.

How to Get Your Body Back into Shape after Childbirth the Way All the Taut-Bodied Entertainment Personalities Such As Jane Fonda Do

Don't kid yourself. Those women have never had babies. Their children were all borne by professional stunt women.

Chapter 8

The First Six Months

Baby's Development during the First Six Months

The first six months is a time of incredibly rapid development for your baby. It will learn to smile, to lift its head, to sit, to play the cello, and to repair automatic transmissions.

Ha ha. Just kidding here, poking a little fun at new parents who watch like hawks for their babies to pass the Major Milestones of Infant Development, when the truth is that during the first six months babies mainly just lie around and poop. They haven't even developed brains at this point. If you were to open up a baby's head—and I am not for a moment suggesting that you should—you would find nothing but an enormous drool gland.

Nevertheless, this is definitely the time to buy your baby its first computer. It's never too soon to start learning about computers,

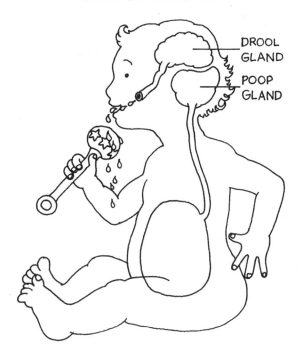

BASIC INFANT ANATOMY

DROOL GLAND

POOP GLAND

as you know if you have been watching those television commercials wherein children whose parents didn't buy them computers at an early age wind up as ragpickers with open sores all over their bodies.

Computers are the way of the future. You can buy them at K-Mart, for God's sake. You see families wandering through the computer department, clutching K-Mart purchases such as huge bags of caramel popcorn manufactured in Korea, and they're saying things like, "I think we should get this computer, because it has a built-in modem and the software support is better." These are not nuclear physicists talking this way; these are K-Mart shoppers, and if they know about computers, your kid damn well better know about them, too.

What kind of computer is best for a baby aged 0 to 6 months? There are many models, ranging widely in memory size, telecommunications facilities, and expansion capabilities, but the critical thing is that your baby's computer should be red, and it should have no sharp edges. Also, you should immediately cut off the plug, because otherwise your baby could receive a dangerous electrical shock from drooling on the keyboard.

Disciplining a New Baby

During the 1950s and 60s, parents were told to be permissive with their children, and the result was juvenile delinquency, drug abuse, Watergate, Pac-Man, California, etc. So we experts now feel you should start disciplining your baby immediately after birth. At random intervals throughout the day, you should stride up to your baby and say, in a strict voice, "There will be no slumber party for *you* tonight, young lady."

You may think this is a waste of time, but scientists have determined that babies as young as three days old can tell, just from the tone of an adult's voice, when they are being told they can't go to a slumber party. You should keep up this tough discipline until your child is in junior high school and thus has access to weapons.

Baby-Tending for Men

During the first six months, your baby will need more care than at any other time in its life except the following 30 months. We modern sensitive husbands realize that it's very unfair to place the entire child-care burden on our wives, so many of us are starting to assume maybe three percent of it. Even this is probably too much. I know I'll be accused of being sexist for saying this, but the typical man has had his nurturing instincts obliterated by watching professional football, and consequently he has no concept of how to tend a baby. He feels he's

A FATHER'S PRIMER

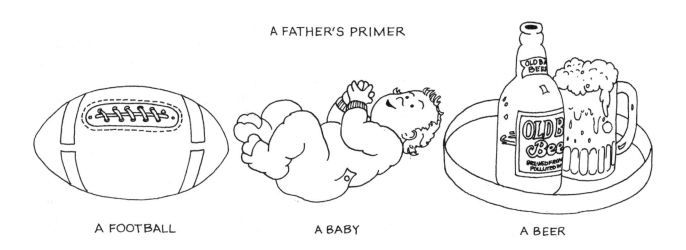

A FOOTBALL   A BABY   A BEER

done a terrific job if the baby isn't stolen by gypsies. You'd get better infant care from an affectionate dog.

But men keep reading articles in the newspaper Style section about how they're supposed to help. So what happens is the family goes to, say, a picnic, and on the way the man, feeling magnanimous, says, "I'll take care of the baby, honey. You just relax and enjoy yourself." So they get to the picnic, and the husband, feeling very proud of himself, tends to the baby by poking it affectionately in the stomach every 45 minutes on his way to the cooler for a new beer. Between pokes the wife comes over maybe 35 times to change the baby's diaper, feed it, cuddle it, arrange its blanket, put the pacifier back in its mouth, brush enormous stinging insects off it, etc.

On the way home, the man remarks on how easy the baby is to take care of, how it hardly cried at all, etc., and the woman plunges the red-hot car cigarette lighter deep into his right thigh. This is bad for a relationship.

So what I've done, men, is I've prepared a little automotive-style maintenance chart for you to follow when you're in charge of the baby.

Men's Baby-Maintenance Chart

INTERVAL	MAINTENANCE ACTIVITY
Every 5 minutes	Lean over baby and state the following in a high-pitched voice: "Yes! We're a *happy* boy or girl! Yes we *are*! Watcha watcha watcha!"
Every 10 minutes	Check all orifices for emerging solids and liquids; wipe and change containment garments as needed
Every 30 minutes	Attempt feeding and burping procedures
Every 60 minutes	Examine entire baby surface for signs of redness, flaking, major eye boogers, etc.
Every 2 hours	Call pediatrician about something

Advice to Women about Babies and Jobs

If you're like many young mothers who held jobs before childbirth, you face a cruel dilemma: Your family could really use another income, yet you feel strongly that you should stay home for at least the first few critical years.

The solution to this dilemma is to have your *baby* get a job. Under federal law, it is now illegal for employers to discriminate against any person solely because that person is a baby. And to their surprise, many employers are finding that babies often make excellent employees, the kind who are always at their desks and never make personal telephone calls. In fact, one major corporation now shows all of its financial proposals to a team of handpicked babies: If they cry at a proposal, it is rejected out of hand; if they attempt to eat it, it is sent on to the board of directors.

What kind of job should you seek for your baby? Your best bet is the kind of job that even the most pathetic incompetent can handle:

State legislator

Paperweight

Consultant

Anything in marketing

Vice president of anything

Clerk in a state motor vehicle bureau

Choosing a Pediatrician

You should choose your pediatrician carefully, for his job is to examine your baby, give it shots, weigh it, measure it—in short, to do everything except attend to the baby when it is actually sick. When the baby is sick, either you or your pediatrician will be on vacation. This is an immutable law of nature.

Babysitters

The best babysitters, of course, are the baby's grandparents. You feel completely comfortable entrusting your baby to them for long periods, which is why most grandparents flee to Florida at the earliest opportunity.

If no grandparents are available, you will have to rent a teenager. You don't want a modern teenager, the kind that hangs around the video-game arcade smoking Marlboros and contracting herpes. No, you want an old-fashioned, responsible teenager, the kind who attends Our Lady of Maximum Discomfort High School and belongs to the 4-H Club and wants to be a nun. Even then you don't want to take any chances. The first time she takes care of your baby, you should never actually leave the house. Drive your car until it's out of sight, then sneak back and crouch in the basement, listening for signs of trouble. In later visits, as you gain confidence in the sitter, you should feel free to eat sandwiches in the basement, and maybe even listen to the radio quietly. After all, this is your night out!

A GOOD BABYSITTER   A BAD BABYSITTER

Safety Tip

Be sure to leave the babysitter a first-aid kit with tourniquet; the phone numbers of the pediatrician, the ambulance, the fire department, the police, the Poison Control Center, all your neighbors, the Mayo Clinic, all your relatives, the State Department, etc; and a note telling her where you are ("We're in the basement") and what to do in the event of an emergency ("Pound on the floor").

Songs for New Babies

One fun thing to do with a small baby while it's lying around is to sing it the traditional baby songs, the ones your mother sang when you were a baby. The words sometimes seem strange to us now, because your mother learned them from her mother, who learned them from her mother, and so on back to medieval England, when most people had the intelligence of kelp. Here are three of my favorites:

LADYBUG
(Robert Frost)

Ladybug, Ladybug
Fly away home
Your children are all burned
They look like charred Raisinets

(Tickle baby under chin.)

HEG-A-LEG MOLLY
(Anonymous)

Heg-a-leg Molly
Daddy's got a bunting
Why do you sleep so soon?
Wet his bed
And he broke his head
And Myron has gone to Vermont.

(Hold baby up and laugh as if you have just said something immensely amusing.)

LAND OF 1,000 DANCES
(Cannibal and the Headhunters)

I said a na
Na na na na
Na na na na na na na na na na
Na na na na

(Check baby's diaper.)

Three Traditional Baby Games

OKLAHOMA BABY CHICKEN HAT

Grasp your baby firmly and place it on your head, stomach side down, then stride about the room, bouncing on the balls of your feet and clucking to the tune of "Surrey with the Fringe on Top."

HERE COMES THE BABY EATER

Place your baby on the carpet, face up, then crawl around on all fours and announce, "I'm so *hungry!* I could eat a *baby!*" Then crawl over and gobble up the baby, starting at the feet, and periodically raising your head and shouting, "Great baby! Delicious!" Babies love this game, but you don't want to play it when other grown-ups are around, because they will try to take custody away from you.

ATTACK OF THE SPACE BABIES

Lie on your back on the floor and hold your baby over you, face down. Move the baby around in the manner of a hovering spacecraft while making various high-pitched science fiction noises such as "BOOOOOOOOWEEEEEEEEOOOOO." Feign great fear as the baby attempts to land on the planet Earth. (NOTE: Wear protective clothing, as space babies often try to weaken the earth's resistance by spitting up on it.)

Babies and Pets

First of all, get rid of your cat. Cats are scum. You've read newspaper stories about elderly widows who die and leave their entire estates to their pet cats, right? Well, your cat reads those stories too, and has spent most of its skulking, devious little life dreaming about inheriting all your money. You know where it goes when it disappears for hours at a time? Investment seminars, that's where.

So if you bring a baby into the home, the cat will see the baby as a rival for your estate and will do anything to turn you against it. Many instances of so-called colic are really nothing more than a cat repeatedly sneaking into a baby's room in the dead of night and jabbing the baby in the stomach.

Dogs, of course, would never do anything like that. They're far too stupid to think of it. So you can keep your dog. In fact, many dogs come to love their masters' babies, often carrying them around gently by the scruffs of their necks, licking them incessantly and refusing to let anybody—even the parents!—near the baby. It's the cutest thing you ever saw, and it really cuts down on child-care costs. Of course, you have to weigh this against the fact that the child

CAT ATTENDING INVESTMENT SEMINAR

develops a tendency to shed and attack squirrels.

DRAWBACK OF CLOSE CHILD-DOG
RELATIONSHIP

Baby Albums

Baby albums are probably the single biggest cause of violent death in America today. The reason is that when people have their first baby, they record everything that happens:

January 5 — Today Rupert is exactly one and a half weeks old! He weighs 8 pounds, 3.587 ounces, up 2.342 ounces from yesterday! He had two poopy diapers today, but definitely not as runny as the ones he had January 3! Also not quite so greenish!

And so on. By the time these people have their *second* baby, they're sick of albums. Oh, they try to slap something together, but it's obvious that their hearts aren't really in it:

1966-74 — Byron was born and is now in the second grade.

So Byron grows up, seemingly normal on the outside, but knowing on the inside that he has this pathetic scrawny album while his brother's looks like the Manhattan telephone directory, and eventually he runs amok in a dentist's office with a Thompson submachine gun. So if you want to do a baby album, fine, go ahead, but have the common decency to notify the police first.

Chapter 9

Six Months to a Year

Development during the Second Six Months

During the second six months, your baby will begin to start crawling around looking for hazards. It will start to become aware of the mysteries of language, perhaps even learning to understand simple phrases such as "No!" and "Spit that out!"

Physically, you'll find your baby is getting hardier and more portable now, so that you can more easily take it to restaurants, although you still can't go inside. By now baby should have gotten over early medical problems such as the colic; if not, you should see your pediatrician and get something you can use to kill yourself.

So all in all, you can look forward in the next six months to a period of change and growth, with a 60 percent chance of afternoon or evening thundershowers.

Baby's First Solid Food

We're using the term "food" loosely here. What we're talking about are those nine

their bowel movements. We have enough trouble with the Congress.

How to Feed
Solid Food to a Baby

The key thing is that you should *not* place the food in the baby's mouth. At this stage, babies use their mouths exclusively for chewing horrible things that they find on the floor (see below). The way they eat food

CIGAR BUTT

CHEWING TOBACCO WAD

CRUSHED PAPER TISSUE

CRUSHED COCKROACH

zillion little jars on the supermarket shelf with the smiling baby on the label and names like "Prunes with Mixed Leeks." Babies hate this stuff. Who wouldn't? It looks like frog waste.

Babies are people, too; they want to eat what *you* want to eat. They want cheeseburgers and beer. If we simply fed them normal diets, they'd eat like crazy. They'd weigh 150 pounds at the end of the first year. This is exactly why we don't feed them normal diets: The last thing we need is a lot of 150-pound people with no control over is by absorbing it directly into their bloodstreams through their faces. So the most efficient way to feed a baby is to smear the food on its chin.

Unfortunately, many inexperienced parents insist on putting food into the baby's mouth. They put in spoonful after spoonful of, say, beets, sincerely believing they are doing something constructive, when in fact the beets are merely going around the Baby Food-Return Loop (see diagram), which all

humans are equipped with until the age of 18 months. After the parents finish "feeding" the baby, they remove the bib and clean up the area, at which point the baby starts to spew beets from its mouth under high pressure, like a miniature beet volcano, until its face is covered with beets, which it can then absorb.

What to Do When a Baby Puts a Horrible Thing in Its Mouth

The trick is to distract the baby with something even worse than what's in its mouth. Next time you're in a bus station rest room, scour the floor for something really disgusting that might appeal to a baby. Stick it in your freezer, so you can quickly defrost it in a microwave oven (allow about 40 seconds) and wave it enticingly in front of the baby until the baby spits out its horrible thing and lunges for yours.

Of course, as your baby catches on to your tricks, you'll need new and different things to entice it with, which means you'll have to spend a great deal of time on your hands and knees in bus station rest rooms. This is a perfectly normal part of being a responsible parent. Remember to say that when the police come.

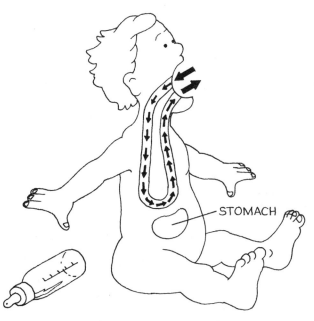

THE BABY FOOD-RETURN LOOP

STOMACH

TEACHING BABY TO SWIM

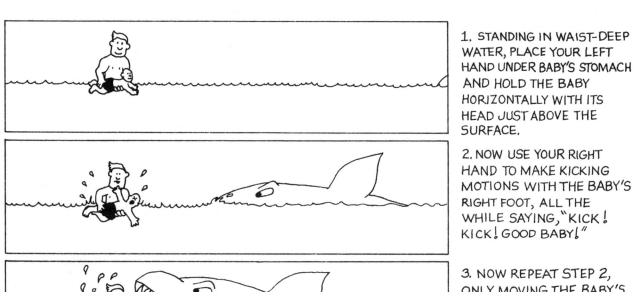

1. STANDING IN WAIST-DEEP WATER, PLACE YOUR LEFT HAND UNDER BABY'S STOMACH AND HOLD THE BABY HORIZONTALLY WITH ITS HEAD JUST ABOVE THE SURFACE.

2. NOW USE YOUR RIGHT HAND TO MAKE KICKING MOTIONS WITH THE BABY'S RIGHT FOOT, ALL THE WHILE SAYING, "KICK! KICK! GOOD BABY!"

3. NOW REPEAT STEP 2, ONLY MOVING THE BABY'S LEFT FOOT.

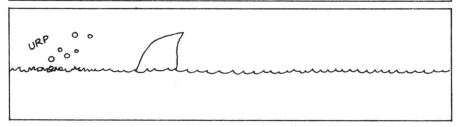

4. NOW RELEASE THE BABY'S FOOT AND URGE IT TO KICK BY ITSELF. BE PATIENT, AND BE SURE TO PRAISE IT LAVISHLY FOR SUCCESS!

Traveling with Baby

By now you're probably thinking how nice it would be to take a trip somewhere and stay in a place where there isn't a hardened yellowish glaze consisting of bananas mixed with baby spit smeared on every surface below a height of two feet. Great idea! My wife and I took many trips with our son, Robert, when he was less than a year old, and we found them all to be surprisingly carefree experiences right up until approximately four hours after we left home, which is when his temperature would reach 106 degrees Fahrenheit. Often we didn't even have to take his temperature, because we could see that his pacifier was melting.

Almost all babies contain a virus that activates itself automatically when the baby is 200 miles or more from its pediatrician. The first time this happened to Robert, we wound up in a pediatric clinic where the doctor got his degree from the University of Kuala Lumpur Medical School and Textile College. He said, "Baby very hot! Bad hot! Could have seezhah!" And we said, "Oh no! My God! Not seezhah!" Then we said, "What the hell is 'seezhah'?" We were afraid it was some kind of horrible Asian disease. Then the doctor rolled his eyes back in his head and went, "Aaaarrgh," and we said, "Oh! *Seizure!*"

The lesson to be learned from this is that when you travel with a baby, you must be prepared for emergencies. Let's say you're planning a trip to the seashore. Besides baby's usual food, formula, bottles, sterilizer, medicine, clothing, diapers, reams of moist towelettes, ointments, lotions, powders, pacifier, toys, portable crib, blankets, rectal thermometer, car seat, stroller, backpack, playpen, and walker, don't forget to take:

- One of those things that look like miniature turkey basters that you use to clear out babies' noses, for when your baby develops a major travel cold and sounds like a little cauldron of mucus gurgling away in the motel room six feet away from you all night long.

- A potent infant-formula anti-cholera drug, for when you're lying on the beach and look up to discover that baby has become intimately involved with an enormous buried dog dropping.

- Something to read while you're sitting in the emergency ward waiting room.

- Plenty of film, so you can record these and the many other hilarious adventures you're bound to have traveling with a baby. You might also take a camera.

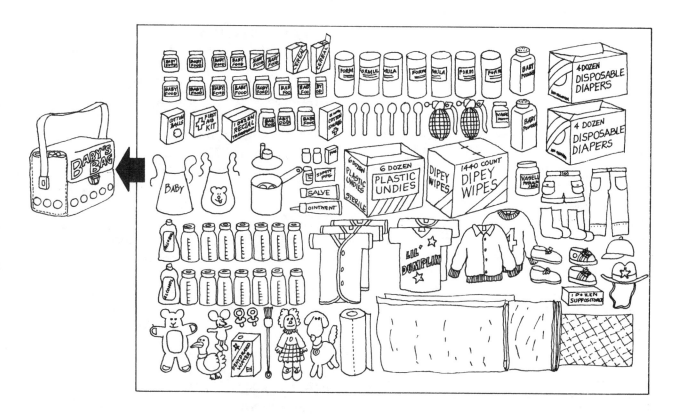

Taking a Baby on an Airplane

First, you should notify the airline in advance that you will be traveling with an infant, so they can use their computers to assign you a seat where your baby will be in a position to knock a Bloody Mary into the lap of a corporate executive on his way to make an important speech.

Also, you should be aware that your baby will insist on standing up in your lap all the way through the flight, no matter how long it is. If you plan to fly with a baby to Japan, all I can say is you'd better have thighs of steel.

Some people try to get their babies to sit down on flights, by giving them sedatives. On our doctor's suggestion, we tried this on a cross-country flight, and all it did was make Robert cranky. The only thing that cheered him up was to grab the hair of the man sitting in front of us, who tried to be nice about it, but if you have a nine-month-old child with a melted Hershey bar all over his pudgy little fingers grabbing your hair all the way from sea to shining sea, you'd start to get a little cranky yourself. So I think it might be a good idea if, on flights featuring babies, the airline distributed sedatives to all the adults, except maybe the pilot.

Teething

Teething usually begins on March 11 at 3:25 P.M., although some babies are off by as much as 20 minutes. The major symptom of teething is that your baby becomes irritable and cries a lot. Of course, this is also the major symptom of everything else, so you

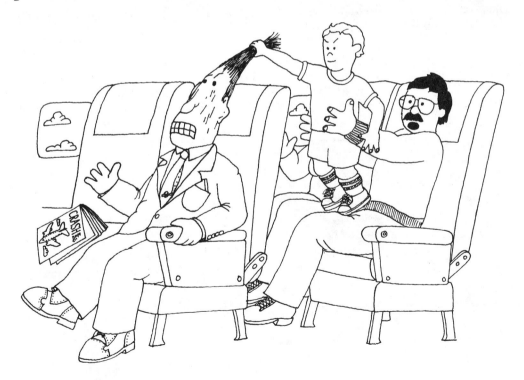

Quick-Reference Baby Medical-Emergency Chart

SYMPTOM	CAUSE	TREATMENT
Baby is chewing contentedly	Baby has found something horrible on floor	Follow enticement procedure described on page 61
Baby is crying	It could be teething, colic, snake bite, some kind of awful rare disease or something	Don't worry: most likely it's nothing
Baby has strange dark lines all over face and body	Baby has gotten hold of laundry marking pen	Wait for baby to grow new skin
Baby's voice sounds muffled	Baby's two-year-old sibling, jealous of all the attention the New Arrival is getting, has covered the New Arrival with dirt	Vacuum baby quickly; explain to sibling that you love him or her just as much as baby, but you will kill him or her if he or she ever does that again

might try the old teething test, which is to stick your finger in baby's mouth and see whether baby bites all the way through to your bone, indicating the presence of teeth.

Most teething babies want to chew on something, so it's a good idea to keep a plastic teething ring in the freezer, taking care not to confuse it with the frozen horrible things from bus station rest rooms (see above).

The first teeth to appear will be the central divisors, followed by the bovines, the colons, the insights, and the Four Tops, for a total of 30 or 40 in all. Your pediatrician will advise you to brush and floss your baby's teeth daily, but he's just kidding.

Chapter 10

The Second Year

Major Developments during the Second Year

Your baby will learn to walk and talk, but that's nothing. The major development is that your baby will learn how to scream for no good reason in shopping malls.

What to Do when a One-Year-Old Starts Screaming in a Shopping Mall, and the Reason Is That You Won't Let It Eat the Pizza Crust That Somebody, Who Was Probably Diseased, Left in the Public Ashtray amid the Sand and the Saliva-Soaked Cigar Butts, but the Other Shoppers Are Staring at You as if to Suggest That You Must Be Some Kind of Heartless Child-Abusing Nazi Scum

First of all, forget about reason. You can't reason with a one-year-old. In fact, reasoning with children of any age has been greatly overrated. There is no documented case of any child being successfully reasoned with before the second year of graduate school.

Also you can't hit a one-year-old. It will just cry harder, and women the age of your mother will walk right up and whap you with their handbags. So what do you do when your child decides to scream in pub-

lic? Here are several practical, time-tested techniques:

■ Explain your side to the other shoppers. As they go by, pull them aside, show them the pizza crust, and talk it over with them, adult to adult ("Look! The little cretin wants to *eat* this! Ha ha! Isn't that CRAZY?").

■ Threaten to take your child to see Santa Claus if it doesn't shut up. All children are born with an instinctive terror of Santa Claus.

■ Let your child have the damn pizza crust. I mean, there's always a chance the previous owner wasn't diseased. It could have been a clergyman or something.

Walking

Most babies learn to walk at about 12 months, although nobody has ever figured out why they bother, because for the next 12 months all they do is stagger off in random directions until they trip over dust molecules and fall on their butts. You cannot catch them before they fall. They fall so quickly that the naked adult eye cannot even see them. This is why diapers are made so thick.

During this phase, your job, as parent, is to trail along behind your child everywhere, holdings your arms out in the Standard Toddler-Following Posture made popular by Boris Karloff in the excellent parent-education film *The Mummy,* only with a degree of hunch approaching that of Neanderthal Man (see diagram) so you'll be able to pick your child up quickly after it falls, because the longer it stays on the ground the more likely it is to find something to put in its mouth.

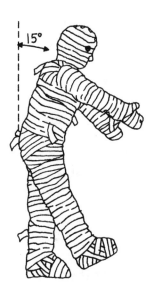

THE MUMMY
(ANGLE OF HUNCH: 15°)

MODERN MAN
(ANGLE OF HUNCH: 30°)

TODDLER

NEANDERTHAL MAN
(ANGLE OF HUNCH: 45°)

Talking

There are two distinct phases in the baby's language development. The second phase is when the baby actually starts talking, which is at about 18 months. The first phase is when the parents imagine that the baby is talking, which is somewhere around 12 months, or even earlier if it's their first baby.

What happens is that one day the baby is holding a little plastic car, trying to get it all the way into his mouth, and he makes some typical random baby sound such as "gawa-noo," and the parents, their brains softened from inhaling Johnson's Baby Oil fumes, say to each other: "Did you hear that? Teddy said 'car'!!!!!" If you've ever been around young parents going through this kind of self-delusion, you know how deranged they can get:

YOU: So! How's little Jason?
PARENT: Talking up a storm! Listen!
JASON: Poomwah arrr grah.
PARENT: Isn't that incredible!
YOU: Ah. Yes. Hmmm.
PARENT: I mean, 13 months old, and already he's concerned about restrictions on imported steel!
YOU: Ah.
JASON: Brrrrrooooooooooooooooooooper.
PARENT: No, Jason, I believe that was during the Kennedy administration.

Eventually, your child will start to learn some real words, which means you'll finally find out what he's thinking. Not much, as it turns out. The first words our son, Robert, said were "dog" and "hot," and after that he didn't seem the least bit interested in learning any more. For the longest time, our conversations went like this:

ME: Look, Robert. See the birds?
ROBERT: Dog.
ME: No, Robert. Those are birds.
ROBERT: Dog dog dog dog dog dog dog dog dog.
ME: Those are *birds,* Robert. Can you say "bird?"
ROBERT (emphatically): Dog dog dog dog dog dog dog dog dog dog dog dog dog dog dog dog dog dog.
ME (giving up): Okay. Those are dogs.
ROBERT: Hot.

Sometimes we'd think we were making real progress on the language front. I remember once my wife called me into the living room, all excited. "Watch this," she said. "Robert, where's your head?" And by God, Robert pointed to his head. I was stunned. I couldn't believe what a genius we had on our hands. Then my wife, bursting with pride, said, "Now watch *this.* Robert, where's your foot?" Robert flashed us a brilliant smile of comprehension, pointed to his head, and said, "dog."

Books for One-Year-Olds

The trouble with books for small children is that they all have titles like, *Ted the Raccoon Vists a Condiments Factory* and are so boring that you doze off after two or three pages and run the risk that your child will slide off your lap and sustain a head injury. So what you want to do is get a book that has more appeal for adults, such as, *Passionate Teenage Periodontal Assistants,* then cut out the pages and paste them over the words in your child's book. This way you can maintain your interest while the child looks at the pictures:

YOU (pretending to read out loud): "My, my," said Ted the Raccoon. "These pickles taste good!" Just look at all those pickles, Johnny!

(While Johnny looks at the pickles, you read: "Brad looked up from *U.S. News and World Report* as a blond, full-breasted periodontal assistant swayed into the waiting room on shapely, nylon-sheathed legs. 'My name is Desiree,' she breathed through luscious, pouting lips, 'and if you'll follow me, I'll show you how to operate the Water Pik oral hygiene appliance.' ")

Teaching Small Children to Read

Children are capable of learning to read much earlier than we give them credit for. Why, Mozart was only two years old when he wrote *Moby Dick*!

When our son was about 18 months old, my wife, who has purchased every baby-improvement book ever published, got one called *How to Teach Your Baby to Read.* The chapter headings started out with "Can Babies Learn to Read?" and worked up to "Babies Definitely Can Learn to Read" and finally got around to "If You Don't Teach Your Baby to Read Right Now, You Are Vermin,"

Me, I was dubious. I thought it was better to teach our child not to pull boogers out of his nose and hand them to us as if they were party favors. But my wife gave it the old college try. She did what the book said, which was to write words like DOG in big letters on pieces of cardboard, then show them to Robert and say the words out loud as if she were having a peck of fun. She did this conscientiously for a couple of weeks, three times a day, and then she realized that Robert was paying no attention whatsoever, and her I.Q. was starting to drop, so she stopped.

My theory is that there is a finite amount of intelligence in a family, and you're supposed to gradually transfer it to your children over a period of many years. This is why your parents started to get so stupid just at the time in your life when you were getting really smart.

How to Put a One-Year-Old to Bed

Children at this age move around a lot while they sleep. If we didn't keep them in cribs, they'd be hundreds of miles away by dawn. So the trick is to put the blankets as far as possible from the child, on the theory that eventually the child will crawl under them.

Bedtime Songs

I advise against "Rock-a-Bye Baby," because it's really sick, what with the baby getting blown out of the tree and crashing down with the cradle. Some of those cradles weigh over 50 pounds. A much better song is "Go to Sleep":

Go to sleep
Go to sleep
Go right straight to sleep
And stay asleep until at least 6:30 A.M.

"ROCK-A-BYE BABY"

INCORRECT BLANKET PLACEMENT

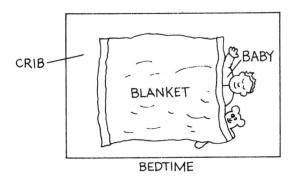

BEDTIME   30 MINUTES LATER

CORRECT BLANKET PLACEMENT

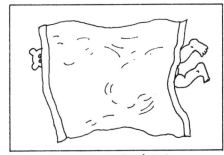

BEDTIME   30 MINUTES LATER

Potty Training

Child psychologists all agree that bodily functions are a source of great anxiety for children, so we can safely assume this isn't true. It certainly wasn't true for our son. He was never happier than when he had a full diaper. We once took him to a department store photographer for baby pictures, and just before we went into the studio, when it was too late to change his diaper, he eliminated an immense quantity of waste, far more than could be explained by any of the known laws of physics. The photographer kept remarking on what a happy baby we had, which was easy for him to say, because he was standing 15 feet away. The pictures all came out swell. In every one, Robert is grinning the insanely happy grin of a baby emitting an aroma that would stun a buffalo. So much for the child's anxiety.

I'll tell you who gets anxious: the parents, that's who. Young parents spend much of their time thinking and talking about their children's bodily functions. You can take an educated, sophisticated couple who, before their child was born, talked about great literature and the true meaning of life, and for the first two years after they become parents, their conversations will center on the consistency of their child's stool, to the point where nobody invites them over for dinner.

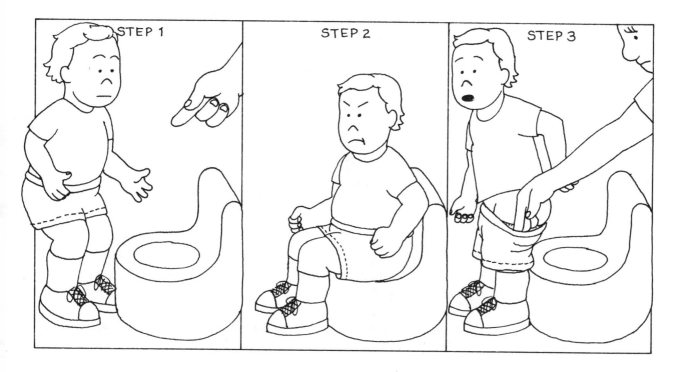

Around the child's second birthday, the parents get tired of waiting for the child to become anxious about his bodily functions, and they decide to give him some anxiety in the form of potty training. This is probably a good thing. A child can go only so far in life without potty training. It is not mere coincidence that six of the last seven presidents were potty trained, not to mention nearly half of the nation's state legislators.

The Traditional Potty Training Technique

The traditional potty training technique is to buy a book written by somebody who was out getting graduate school degrees when his own children were actually being potty trained. My wife bought a book that claimed we could potty train our child in one day, using a special potty that (I swear this

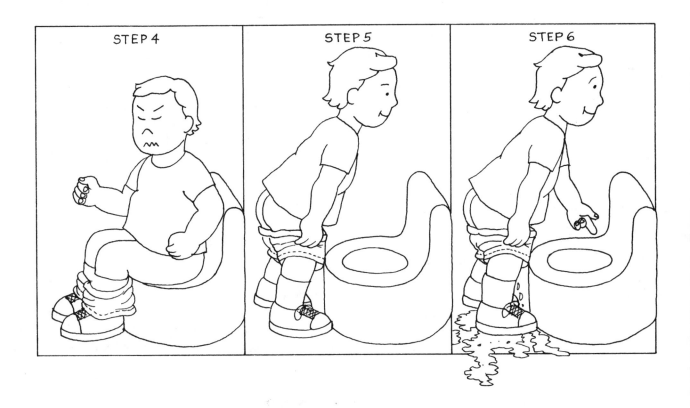

is true) played "Twinkle, Twinkle Little Star" when the child went in it. She also got a little book for our son that explained potty training in terms that a small child could understand, such as "poo-poo."

Now there may well be some parents, somewhere, who managed to potty train their child in one day, but I am willing to bet they used a cattle prod. My wife read that book all the way through, and she did exactly what it said, which was that you should feed your child a lot of salty snacks so that it would drink a lot of liquids and consequently would have to pee about every 20 minutes, which would give it lots of opportunities to practice going in the musical potty, so that it would have the whole procedure nailed down solid by the end of the day. That was the theory.

When I left home that morning, my wife was reading the poo-poo book to Robert. She had a cheerful, determined look on her face. When I got home that evening, more than ten hours later, there were cracker crumbs everywhere, and piles of soiled child's underpants, seemingly hundreds of them, as if the entire junior class of St. Swithan's School for Incontinent Children had been there on a field trip. My wife was still in her nightgown. I don't think she had even brushed her teeth. It is extremely fortunate for the man who wrote the potty

training book that he did not walk in the door with me, because the police would have found his lifeless body lying in the bushes with an enormous bulge in his throat playing "Twinkle, Twinkle Little Star."

We did, in the end, get Robert potty trained. We did it the same way everybody does, the same way you will, by a lot of nagging and false alarms and about 30,000 accidents and endless wildly extravagant praise for bowel movements ("Honey! Come and see what Robert did!" "Oh Robert, that's *wonderful!*" etc.).

The big drawback to potty training is that, for a while, children assume that all adults are as fascinated with it as their parents seem to be. Robert would walk up to strangers in restaurants and announce, "I went pee-pee." And the strangers would say, "Ah." And Robert would say, "I didn't do poop." And the strangers would say, "No?" And Robert would say, "I'm gonna do poop later." And so on.

Nutrition

By the middle of the second year, your baby's Food-Return Loop has disappeared, so its mouth is connected directly to its stomach. At this point, you want to adjust its diet to see that each day it gets food from all three Basic Baby Food Nutrition Groups (see chart). You also should encourage your baby to feed itself, so that you won't have to be in the room.

The Basic Baby Food Nutrition Groups

FOODS THAT BABIES HURL AT THE CEILING

- Anything from jars with babies on the labels
- Anything the baby ate the day before, so you went out and bought $30 worth of it

FOODS THAT BABIES HURL AT THE DOG

- Anything in a weighty container
- Taffy
- Zwieback (NOTE: Zwieback has sharp edges, so the dog should wear protective clothing)

FOODS THAT BABIES EAT

- Anything from vending machines
- Caulking
- Anything with dead ants on it
- Sand

Chapter 11

The Third Year

This period is often referred to as the "terrible twos," not so much because children this age start behaving any worse than before, but because they reach the size where if they swing at you, they'll hit you square in the crotch.

The important thing to remember here is that your child is only trying to establish its independence. This is a necessary part of its development: It must learn to make its own decisions, to interact with the world directly rather than through the protective mediation of its parents. Your child must also learn that when it hits a bigger person in the crotch, it should pretend to be very, very sorry.

How to Discipline a Two-Year-Old

Discipline during this phase consists of choosing the appropriate Escalating Futile Parental Disciplinary Threat. A handy reference chart is printed here for your use.

Remember that when your two-year-old "misbehaves," it's usually becaue of his natural curiosity. It is not cruelty that causes him to thrust a Bic pen deep into the dog's nostril; it is a genuine desire to find out how you will react.

The time-tested way to react is to work your way up the ladder of Traditional Escalating Futile Parental Disciplinary Threats.

The Traditional Escalating Futile Parental Disciplinary Threats

1. "You're going to poke somebody's eye out."
2. "You're going to make me very angry."
3. "You're going straight to your room."
4. "I'm going to tell your father."
5. "I'm going to tell Santa Claus."
6. "I'm not going to give you any dessert."
7. "I'm not going to buy you any more Hot Wheels."
8. "I'm very angry now."
9. "I'm going to give you a good smack."
10. "I mean it."
11. "I really mean it."
12. "I'm not kidding."
13. (SMACK).

NOTE: If there's a real discipline emergency, such as your child has somehow gotten hold of an acetylene torch, you may have to start right in at Threat Number 8.

BABY WITH NORMAL CHILDHOOD FEAR OF GIANT LOBSTERS

Fears

All of us are born with a set of instinctive fears—of falling, of the dark, of lobsters, of falling on a lobster in the dark, of speaking before a Rotary Club, and of the words "Some Assembly Required." These fears help protect your child from real danger, and you should encourage them. ("Run!" you should shout. "Lobsters are coming!")

But many two-year-olds also develop seemingly irrational fears. They get these from Mister Rogers. He tries to reassure his young viewers about standard childhood fears, but the children would never have thought of them if Mister Rogers hadn't brought them up. My son and I once watched Mister Rogers sing this song in

Fears Your Mother Teaches You during Childhood

You needed these fears to become a responsible adult, and now it's time to start passing them on to your child.

- The fear that if you cross your eyes, they'll get stuck that way.

- The fear that if you go in the water less than an hour after eating, you will get a cramp and sink to the bottom, helpless, and possibly catch cold.

- The fear that public toilet seats have germs capable of leaping more than 20 feet.

- The fear that if you wear old underwear, a plane will crash on you and rip your clothes off and your underwear will be broadcast nationally on the evening news. ("The victim shown here wearing the underwear with all the holes and stains has been identified as . . .")

- The fear that if you get in trouble at school, it will go on your Permanent Record and follow you for the rest of your life. ("Your qualifications are excellent, Mr. Barry, but I see here in your Permanent Record that in the eighth grade you and Joseph DiGiacinto flushed a lit cherry bomb down the boys' room toilet at Harold C. Crittenden Junior High School. Frankly, Mr. Barry, we're looking for people with more respect for plumbing than that.")

MR. ROGERS

NOT MR. ROGERS

grits in seconds. Aided by this kind of understanding and support from us, Robert eventually stopped imagining his horse, which was good because it was ruining the carpet.

So unless you want your child to develop a set of irrational fears, I advise you not to let him watch Mister Rogers. A far better alternative is the Saturday morning cartoon shows, which instill the healthy and rational fear that evil beings with sophisticated weapons are trying to destroy the planet.

Toys for Two-Year-Olds

Pay no attention to the little statements on the boxes that say things like "For Ages 1 to 3." If you heed these statements, all you'll buy for the first few years are little plastic shapes that the child is supposed to put in corresponding little holes, which is so exceedingly boring that after five minutes the child will develop an ear infection just for a change of pace. The best toys for a child aged 0 to 3 is a toy that says "For Ages 10 to 14." The best toy for a child aged 10 to 14 is cash, or its own apartment.

You should also buy Fisher-Price toys. Not for your child. For your own protection. Every Fisher-Price toy has been approved by a panel consisting of dozens of child

which he said over and over, in the most cheerful voice imaginable, that "You can never go down the drain." By the time he finished, we were both very concerned about going down the drain. And this came at a time when I had just gotten over the fear of being stabbed to death in the shower, which I got from *Psycho*.

Recently, my son became convinced that a horse was coming into his bedroom at night to get him. The way to cope with this kind of fear is to allow the child to confront it openly. We took Robert to visit some real horses, so he could see for himself that they are nothing more than huge creatures with weird eyeballs and long teeth and hard feet that could stomp him to the consistency of psychologists and pediatricians and Ralph Nader and Mister Rogers, and in most states failure to own at least a half dozen of these toys is considered legal proof of child abuse.

Another reason why you should buy Fisher-Price toys is that they are built better than any other products you can buy, even in Japan. They're made out of some plastic-like substance that Fisher-Price imports from another planet, and nothing can harm it. If Fisher-Price had any marketing sense, it would make its cars much bigger and put real engines in them and change the seats so that real people could sit in them. Right now, the seats are designed for little toy ball-headed Fisher-Price people, which have no arms or legs (the Fisher-Price factory employees whack off the arms and legs with little machetes just before shipment). Consumers would snork these cars up like hotcakes. We'd forget all about Toyota.

How to Hold a Birthday Party for Two-Year-Olds

Not in your house. Outdoors, I don't care if you live in Juneau, Alaska, and it's January. You want to hold it outdoors, and you want the fire department to stand by to hose the area down immediately after you put the ice cream in front of them. And you want all the adults inside the house where they can drink in relative safety.

A Word about Smurfs, Snoopy, Strawberry Shortcake, and All the Other Nauseating Little Characters That You Swear You Will Never Allow in Your Home

Forget it. These toys are creatures of the multibillion-dollar Cuteness Industry, which is extremely powerful and has

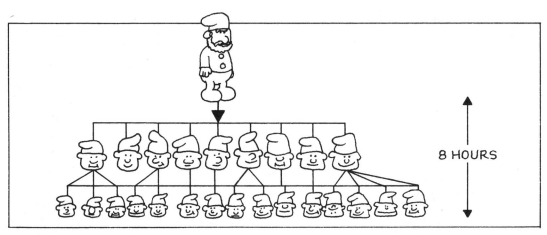

OVERNIGHT REPRODUCTION RATE OF OBNOXIOUS TOYS

8 HOURS

influence everywhere. The *Voyager II* space probe found traces of a Snoopy toothbrush on Mars. If you fail to buy Smurfs, agents of the Smurf Corporation will mail them to you, or smuggle them into your house baked inside loaves of bread, until you reach the national average of 24 Smurfs per child under eight.

So you have to live with them. The only defense you have is to encourage your child to play hostile games with them, such as "Smurf War Tribunal" and "Mr. Smurf Visits the Toaster Oven."

Questions

Starting at around age two, your child will start asking you a great many questions. This can be annoying, but you must remem-ber that if children couldn't ask questions, they would have no way to irritate you when they're strapped in the car seat.

The most popular question for small children is "Why?" They can use it anywhere, and it's usually impossible to answer:

CHILD: What's that?
YOU: That's a goat.
CHILD: Why?

Our son would lie awake at night thinking of questions that nobody could answer:

ROBERT: Which is bigger, five or six?
ME (confidently): Six.
ROBERT: What if it's a great big five made out of stone?
ME: Um.
ROBERT: And a little six made out of wood.

Once I hauled out my guitar to sing traditional folk songs to Robert. It was going to be togetherness. It was going to be meaningful. It was going to be just like on "The Waltons." Here is a verbatim transcript:

ME (singing): "Puff, the Magic Dragon, lived by the sea . . ."
ROBERT: What's a dragon?
ME: It's a great big animal that has fire coming out of its nose. (Singing) "Little Jackie Paper, loved that rascal . . ."
ROBERT: Did Jackie Paper have fire coming out of his nose?
ME: No, he was a little boy, like you. Do you have fire coming out of your nose?
ROBERT (thoughtfully): No. Boogies.
ME: Um. Right. (Singing) "Little Jackie Paper, loved that . . ."
ROBERT: Did Jackie Paper have boogies coming out of his nose?

The point here is that your child will never ask you where babies come from, or why the sky is blue, or any other question that has a real answer. Your child is going to want to know whether Jackie Paper had boogies coming out of his nose, and whether you answer "yes" or "no," your child will want to know why.

Preschool Programs

Near the end of the second year, most parents start thinking about putting their child in a preschool program, which is a place that has all these little tables and chairs where your child makes these pathetic drawings that you put on your refrigerator. Also they eat snacks and take naps. That's the core of the curriculum.

You must choose your child's preschool program carefully, because it determines how well the child does in kindergarten, which affects how well the child does in grade school, which is an important factor in how well the child does in junior high school, which forms the basis for how well the child does in high school, which of course determines which college the child gets into.

On the other hand, all the child will do in college is listen to loud music and get ready for dates, so you don't have to be all *that* careful about choosing the preschool program. Just kick the little chairs a few times to make sure they're sturdy, and say a few words to the staff to let them know you're a Concerned Parent ("Anything happens to my kid, I come in here and break some thumbs. Got it?").

Also, make sure the preschool doesn't have any guinea pigs. I don't know why, but somewhere along the line, preschool educators picked up the insane notion that guinea pigs are educational, when in fact all they do is poop these little pellets that look exactly like the pellets you give them to eat. You don't want your child exposed to that.

The Little Boy and the Toad (A Child-Participation Bedtime Story)

It's good to encourage your child to participate in making up stories. Here's a bedtime story I used to tell Robert, with his help:

ME: Once upon a time, there was a little boy named John.
ROBERT: No. Lee.

ME: Okay. There was a little boy named Lee, and one day he was walking along, and he . . .
ROBERT: No. He was driving.
ME: Okay, he was driving along, and he saw . . .
ROBERT: In a Jeep.
ME: He was driving along in a Jeep, and he saw a little toad.
ROBERT: No. He saw a dump truck.
ME: And they all lived happily ever after. Now go to sleep.
ROBERT: Why?

Epilogue:
Should You Have Another?

Well! So here we are! We've taken your baby from a little gourdlike object with virtually no marketable skills to a real little human being, capable of putting the cat in the dryer and turning it on all by himself or herself!

Sure, it's been a lot of work for you. Sure, you would have liked to have had a few more quiet evenings alone, just the two of you sipping wine and talking instead of sitting in the hospital X-ray department, waiting to find out whether your child had, in fact, swallowed the bullets that it snatched out of the belt of the policeman who was writing a traffic ticket because you smashed into the furniture store when your child threw your glasses out the car window. But take a minute to look at the positive side of parenthood.

(Pause)

Give it time. You'll come up with something. And when you do, think about how much fun it would be to do the whole thing over again. Not with the same child, of course; there is no way you could get it back into the uterus. I'm talking about a completely new baby, only this time around you'll have a chance to avoid the mistakes you made last time, such as labor. I understand from reading the publications sold at supermarket checkout counters that you can now have a baby in a test tube! I don't know the details, but it sounds much less painful than the usual route, although you'd have to balance that against the fact that the baby would be extremely small and cylindrical. It would look like those little Fisher-Price people.

But whether you have another child or not, the important thing is that you've experienced the fulfillment that comes with being a parent. You may feel your efforts will never be rewarded, but believe me, you have sown the seeds of love and trust, and I guarantee you that there will come a time, years from now, when your child—now an adult with children of his or her own—will come to you, and, in a voice quaking with emotion, ask for a loan for a down payment on a house much nicer than yours.

Index